NATIONAL GEOGRAPHIC LEARNING READER

AF713722

biological anthropology

NATIONAL GEOGRAPHIC LEARNING | CENGAGE Learning

Biological Anthropology

© 2014 National Geographic Learning, Cengage Learning

ALL RIGHTS RESERVED. No part of this work covered by the copyright herein may be reproduced, transmitted, stored, or used in any form or by any means graphic, electronic, or mechanical, including but not limited to photocopying, recording, scanning, digitizing, taping, web distribution, information networks, or information storage and retrieval systems, except as permitted under Section 107 or 108 of the 1976 United States Copyright Act, without the prior written permission of the publisher.

National Geographic and the Yellow Border are registered trademarks of the National Geographic Society.

Photographic Credit: cover
© Frans Lanting/National Geographic Image Collection

For product information and technology assistance, contact us at
Cengage Learning Customer & Sales Support, 888-915-3276

For permission to use material from this text or product,
submit all requests online at **www.cengage.com/permissions.**
Further permissions questions can be emailed to
permissionrequest@cengage.com.

ISBN: 978-12851-94479

National Geographic Learning
1880 Oak Avenue, Suite 300
Evanston, IL 60201
USA

Cengage Learning products are represented in Canada by Nelson Education, Ltd.

Visit National Geographic Learning online at **NGL.cengage.com**
Visit our corporate website at **www.cengage.com.**

Printed in the USA.
RR Donnelley, Jefferson City, MO

12 13 14 15 16 17 18 19 20 21 22

10 9 8 7 6 5 4 3 2 1

Table *of* Contents

© 1900 CHRIS JOHNS/National Geographic Image Collection

About the Series

Cengage Learning and National Geographic Learning are proud to present the *National Geographic Learning Reader Series*. This groundbreaking series is brought to you through an exclusive partnership with the National Geographic Society, an organization that represents a tradition of amazing stories, exceptional research, first-hand accounts of exploration, rich content, and authentic materials.

The series brings learning to life by featuring compelling images, media, and text from National Geographic. Through this engaging content, students develop a clearer understanding of the world around them. Published in a variety of subject areas, the *National Geographic Learning Reader Series* connects key topics in each discipline to authentic examples and can be used in conjunction with most standard texts or online materials available for your courses.

How the reader works

Each article is focused on one topic relevant to the discipline. The introduction provides context to orient students and focus questions that suggest ideas to think about while reading the selection. Rich photography, compelling images, and pertinent maps are amply used to further enhance understanding of the selections. The chapter culminating section includes discussion questions to stimulate both in-class discussion and out-of-class work.

An eBook will accompany each reader and will provide access to the text online with a media library that may include images, videos, and other content specific to each individual discipline.

Few organizations present this world, its people, places, and precious resources in a more compelling way than National Geographic. Through this reader series we honor the mission and tradition of National Geographic Society: to inspire people to care about the planet.

Preface

Physical anthropology, also referred to as biological anthropology, is the study of human origins and the evolution of our species through the analysis of physical remains. As a sub-field of anthropology, physical anthropology draws from multiple disciplines—including, but not limited to, genetics, primatology, human biology, neuroscience, comparative anatomy and physiology, archaeology, forensics, and the social sciences—in piecing together fragmented evidence regarding our deep and recent pasts. Traces left in DNA, fossils, and artifacts clue into the physiological, neurological, environmental, and cultural adaptions of humankind from our infancy as bipedal hominids to our current states as text-messaging *Homo* sapien sapiens.

The rich history of our species is a dynamic one and is frequently subject to revision. As anthropological theories, scientific methods, and technologies grow in sophistication, our understanding of what it means to be human and how we became human can significantly change at the unearthing of new discoveries. As we are all subject to evolutionary forces and selective pressures, physical anthropologists, themselves, are also *subjects* within the narrative of human evolution. While physical anthropologists strive for objectivity and empirically grounded work, personal biases and assumptions are not always easy to avoid. Controversy and skepticism frequently surround the interpretation of physical evidence, within both the scientific and lay communities alike. As such, multiple lines of evidence and reevaluations of old data in light of new data are quite necessary.

This reader simultaneously covers some of the major areas of foci, or sub-disciplines, of physical anthropology (genetics, primatology, and paleoanthropology) and demonstrates the highly contestable nature of interpreting research findings and how new discoveries are challenging dated narratives and ongoing perceptions. For example, articles two and three call into question the parameters of uniquely "Modern Human" behavior, as Fongoli chimps (including females) are fashioning sphere-like hunting tools, and as Neanderthals are being proven to have been capable of language with the FOXP2 gene and of symbolic expression with body adornment and ritual burial practices. Are we anthropomorphizing chimpanzees and debasing Neanderthals? How are perceptions, interpretations, research directions, and scientific designs politically imbued?

Along similar lines of inquiry, the relatively recent discovery of the Flores Island "hobbits," in article four, has the potential to rewrite paleoanthropological history as we know it. If these debatably dwarfed species of *Homo* with small cranial capacities were able to use fire and hunt with sophisticated stone tools, what does this mean of our other small-brained hominid ancestors? And if the ancient migratory patterns of Modern Humans out of Africa (article one) suggest that anatomically Modern Humans were contemporaries of both erectus-like "hobbits" (article four) and Eurasian Neanderthals (article three), were Modern Humans responsible for the extinction of both?

As physical anthropology makes it possible to answer such questions by connecting physical evidence—fossils, DNA, and artifacts—with certain behavioral and cultural adaptations, what insights can it provide for modern *Homo* sapien sapiens? The final and fifth article of the reader ties it all together and provides evolutionary explanations for certain biomechanical flaws (or aches and pains) that ail us as upright moderns. How much of it accounts for "evolutionary trade-offs" and how much of it pertains to our lifestyles?

Each article is followed by discussion questions that engage the material presented by the articles and additional features that seek both your input on ongoing debates and your hands-on collection and analysis of data related to each article topic for your own physical anthropology field journal. It is our hope that the subsequent pages assist you in developing an informed understanding of what physical anthropologists do, the array of methods and techniques they employ in answering a variety of questions regarding the diverse and dynamic evolution of our species, and how you are an integral component of these pursuits.

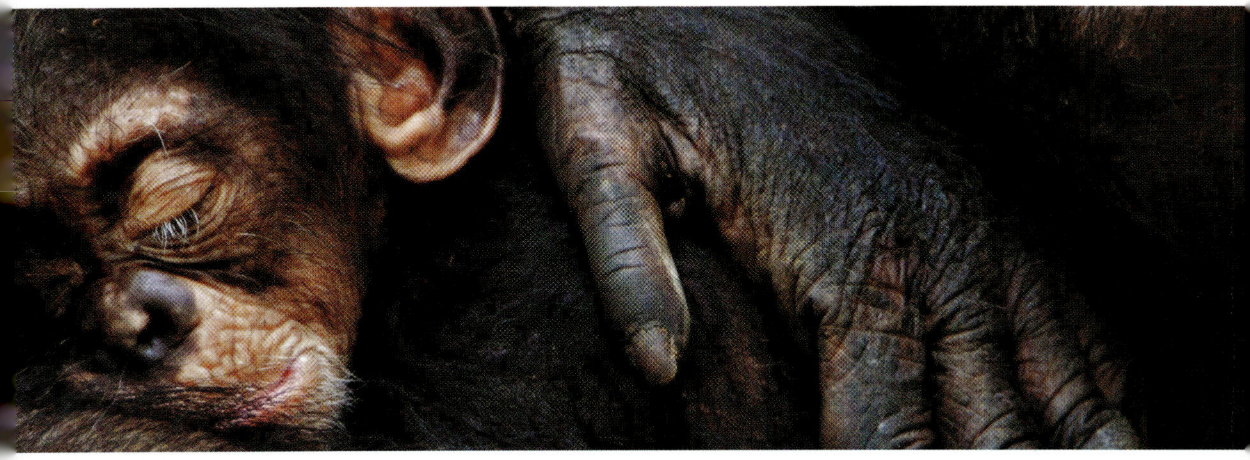

© 2008 FRANS LANTING/National Geographic Image Collection

THE GREATEST JOURNEY

The Greatest Journey traces the ancient migration routes of our Modern Human ancestors out from their origins in Africa to various regions of the world through the mapping of genetic mutations in mitochondrial DNA and the Y chromosome. While human genomic projects can complement patchy hominid fossil evidence in writing our evolutionary history, it is met with opposition grounded in ethical politics.

As you read "The Greatest Journey," consider the following questions:

- How is genetic evidence used to trace probable migration routes of Modern Humans?
- How long ago is it purported that Modern Humans migrated out of the African continent?
- When did Modern Humans start to appear in each continent?
- What are the assets and limitations of human genome projects?
- In what ways are genomic studies opposed?

An Onge man and others like him from the Andaman Islands off Myanmar carry some of the oldest genetic markers found outside Africa—evidence that Homo sapiens, *or modern humans, headed east from Africa as long as 70,000 years ago. Fanning out across the continents, they gave rise to new faces and races.*

© 2006 RAGHUBIR SINGH/National Geographic Image Collection

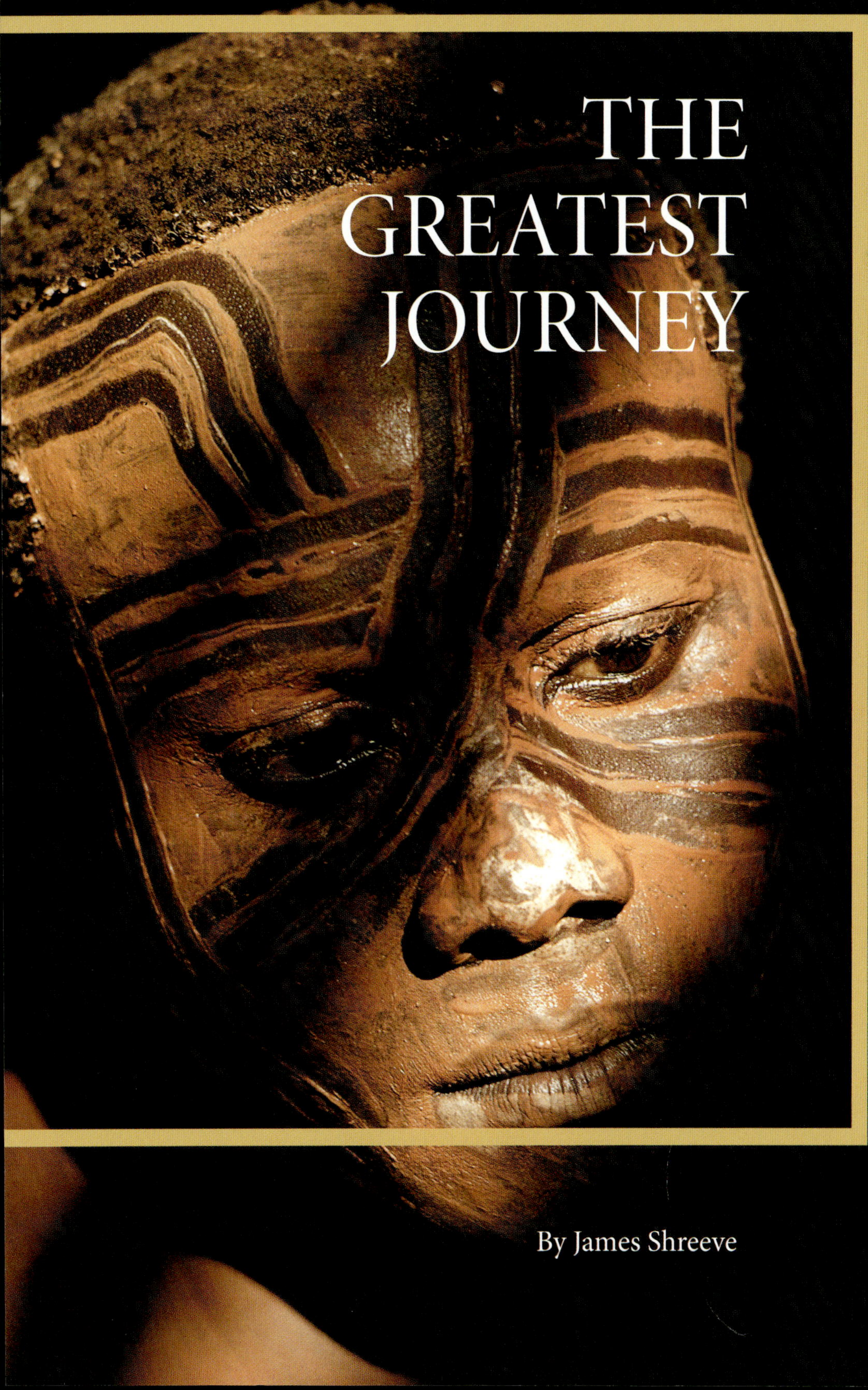

THE GREATEST JOURNEY

By James Shreeve

A desert hunter of the San people, Klaas Kruiper pauses to wait for his family in South Africa's Kalahari Desert. DNA markers common among the San could date back to the origin of modern humans. The San communicate with clicks to keep from spooking game—a feature that is also found in languages spoken by other African groups who carry ancient DNA markers.

© 1900 CHRIS JOHNS/National Geographic Image Collection

THE GENES OF PEOPLE TODAY

TELL OF OUR ANCESTORS' TREK

OUT OF AFRICA TO THE FAR CORNERS OF THE GLOBE.

Everybody loves a good story, and when it's finished, this will be the greatest one ever told. It begins in Africa with a group of hunter-gatherers, perhaps just a few hundred strong. It ends some 200,000 years later with their six and a half billion descendants spread across the Earth, living in peace or at war, believing in a thousand different deities or none at all, their faces aglow in the light of campfires and computer screens.

The human genetic code, or genome, is 99.9 percent identical throughout the world.

In between is a sprawling saga of survival, movement, isolation, and conquest, most of it unfolding in the silence of prehistory. Who were those first modern people in Africa? What compelled a band of their descendants to leave their home continent as little as 50,000 years ago and expand into Eurasia? What routes did they take? Did they interbreed with earlier members of the human family along the way? When and how did humans first reach the Americas?

In sum: Where do we all come from? How did we get to where we are today?

For decades the only clues were the sparsely scattered bones and artifacts our ancestors left behind on their journeys. In the past 20 years, however, scientists have found a record of ancient human migrations in the DNA of living people. "Every drop of human blood contains a history book written in the language of our genes," says population geneticist Spencer Wells, a National Geographic explorer-in-residence.

The human genetic code, or genome, is 99.9 percent identical throughout the world. What's left is the DNA responsible for our individual differences—in eye color or disease risk, for example—as well as some that serves no apparent function at all. Once in an evolutionary blue moon, a random, harmless mutation can occur in one of these functionless stretches, which is then passed down to all of that person's descendants. Generations later, finding that same mutation, or marker, in two people's DNA indicates that they share the same ancestor. By comparing markers in many different populations, scientists can trace their ancestral connections.

In most of the genome, these minute changes are obscured by the genetic reshuffling that

---

Adapted from "The Greatest Journey" by James Shreeve: National Geographic Magazine, March 2006.

© 2006 DAVID EDWARDS/National Geographic Image Collection

MONGOLIA

© 2006 Michael Nichols/National Geographic Image Collection

BRAZIL

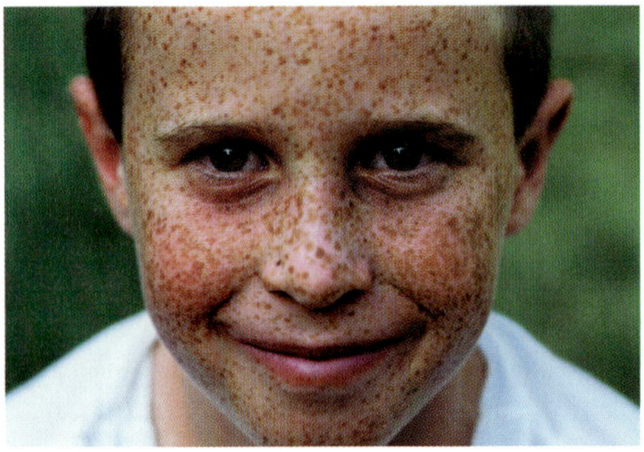
© 2006 JOEL SARTORE/National Geographic Image Collection

UNITED STATES

takes place each time a mother and father's DNA combine to make a child. Luckily a couple of regions preserve the telltale variations. One, called mitochondrial DNA (mtDNA), is passed down intact from mother to child. Similarly, most of the Y chromosome, which determines maleness, travels intact from father to son.

The accumulated mutations in your mtDNA and (for males) your Y chromosome are only two threads in a vast tapestry of people who have contributed to your genome. But by comparing the mtDNA and Y chromosomes of people from various populations, geneticists can get a rough idea of where and when those groups parted ways in the great migrations around the planet.

In the mid-1980s the late Allan Wilson and colleagues at the University of California, Berkeley, used mtDNA to pinpoint humanity's ancestral home. They compared mtDNA from women around the world and found that women of African descent showed twice as much diversity as their sisters. Since the telltale mutations seem to occur at a steady rate, modern humans must have lived in Africa twice as long as anywhere else. Scientists now calculate that all living humans are related to a single woman who lived roughly 150,000 years ago in Africa, a "mitochondrial Eve." She was not the only woman alive at the time, but if geneticists are right, all of humanity is linked to Eve through an unbroken chain of mothers.

Mitochondrial Eve was soon joined by "Y chromosome Adam," an analogous father of us all, also from Africa. Increasingly refined DNA studies have confirmed this opening chapter of our story over and over: All the variously shaped and shaded people of Earth trace their ancestry to African hunter-gatherers.

Looking more closely at DNA markers in Africa, scientists may have found traces of those founders. Ancestral DNA markers turn up most often among the San people of southern Africa and the Biaka Pygmies of central Africa, as well as in some East African tribes. The San and two of the East African tribes also speak languages that feature a repertoire of unique sounds, including clicks. Perhaps these far-flung people pay witness to an expansion of our earliest ancestors within Africa, like the fading ripples from a pebble dropped in a pond.

What seems virtually certain now is that at a remarkably recent date—probably between 50,000 and 70,000 years ago—one small wavelet from Africa lapped up onto the shores of western Asia. All non-Africans share markers carried by those first emigrants, who may have numbered just a thousand people.

What accounts for the ancient wanderlust? Perhaps some kind of neurological mutation led to spoken language and made our ancestors fully modern, setting a small band on course to colonize the world.

Some archaeologists think the migration out of Africa marked a revolution in behavior that also included more sophisticated tools, wider social networks, and the first art and body ornaments. Perhaps some kind of neurological mutation had led to spoken language and made our ancestors fully modern, setting a small band of them on course to colonize the world. But other scientists see finely wrought tools and other traces of modern behavior scattered around Africa long before those first steps outside the continent. "It's not a 'revolution' if it took 200,000 years," says Alison Brooks of George Washington University.

Whatever tools and cognitive skills the emigrants packed with them, two paths lay open into Asia. One led up the Nile Valley, across the Sinai Peninsula, and north into the Levant. But another also beckoned. Seventy thousand years ago the Earth was entering the last ice age, and sea levels were sinking as water was locked up in glaciers. At its narrowest, the mouth of the Red Sea between the Horn of Africa and Arabia would have been only a few miles wide. Using primitive watercraft, modern humans could have crossed over while barely getting their feet wet.

Once in Asia, genetic evidence suggests, the population split. One group stalled temporarily in the Middle East, while the other followed the coast around the Arabian Peninsula, India, and beyond. Each generation may have pushed just a couple of miles farther.

"The movement was probably imperceptible," says Spencer Wells, who heads the National Geographic Society's Genographic Project, a global effort to refine the picture of early migrations. "It was less of a journey and probably more like walking a little farther down the beach to get away from the crowd."

Over the millennia, a few steps a year and a few hops by boat added up. The wanderers had reached southeastern Australia by 45,000 years ago, when a man was buried at a site called Lake Mungo. Artifact-bearing soil layers beneath the burial could be as old as 50,000 years—the earliest evidence of modern humans far from Africa.

No physical trace of these people has been found along the 8,000 miles from Africa to Australia—all may have vanished as the sea rose after the Ice Age. But a genetic trace endures. A few indigenous groups on the Andaman Islands near Myanmar, in Malaysia, and in Papua New Guinea—as well as almost all Australian Aborigines—carry signs of an ancient mitochondrial lineage, a trail of genetic bread crumbs dropped by the early migrants.

People in the rest of Asia and Europe share different but equally ancient mtDNA and Y-chromosome lineages, marking them as descendants of the other, stalled branch of the African exodus. At first, rough terrain and the Ice Age climate blocked further progress. Europe, moreover, was a stronghold of the Neandertals, descendants of a much earlier migration of pre-modern humans out of Africa.

Finally, perhaps 40,000 years ago, modern humans advanced into the Neandertals' territory. Overlapping layers of Neandertal and early modern human artifacts at a cave in France suggest that the two kinds of humans could have met. How these two peoples—the destined parvenu and the *(Continued on page 10)*

① AFRICAN CRADLE

Most paleoanthropologists and geneticists agree that modern humans arose some 200,000 years ago in Africa. The earliest modern human fossils were found in Omo Kibish, Ethiopia. Sites in Israel hold the earliest evidence of modern humans outside Africa, but that group went no farther, dying out about 90,000 years ago.

② OUT OF AFRICA

Genetic data show that a small group of modern humans left Africa for good 70,000 to 50,000 years ago and eventually replaced all earlier types of humans, such as Neandertals. All non-Africans are the descendants of these travelers, who may have migrated around the top of the Red Sea or across its narrow southern opening.

③ THE FIRST AUSTRALIANS

Discoveries at two ancient sites—artifacts from Malakunanja and fossils from Lake Mungo—indicate that modern humans followed a coastal route along southern Asia and reached Australia nearly 50,000 years ago. Their descendants, Australian Aborigines, remained genetically isolated on that island continent until recently.

④ EARLY EUROPEANS

Paleoanthropologists long thought that the peopling of Europe followed a route from North Africa through the Levant. But genetic data show that the DNA of today's western Eurasians resembles that of people in India. It's possible that an inland migration from Asia seeded Europe between 40,000 and 30,000 years ago.

⑤ POPULATING ASIA

Around 40,000 years ago, humans pushed into Central Asia and arrived on the grassy steppes north of the Himalaya. At the same time, they traveled through Southeast Asia and China, eventually reaching Japan and Siberia. Genetic clues indicate that humans in northern Asia eventually migrated to the Americas.

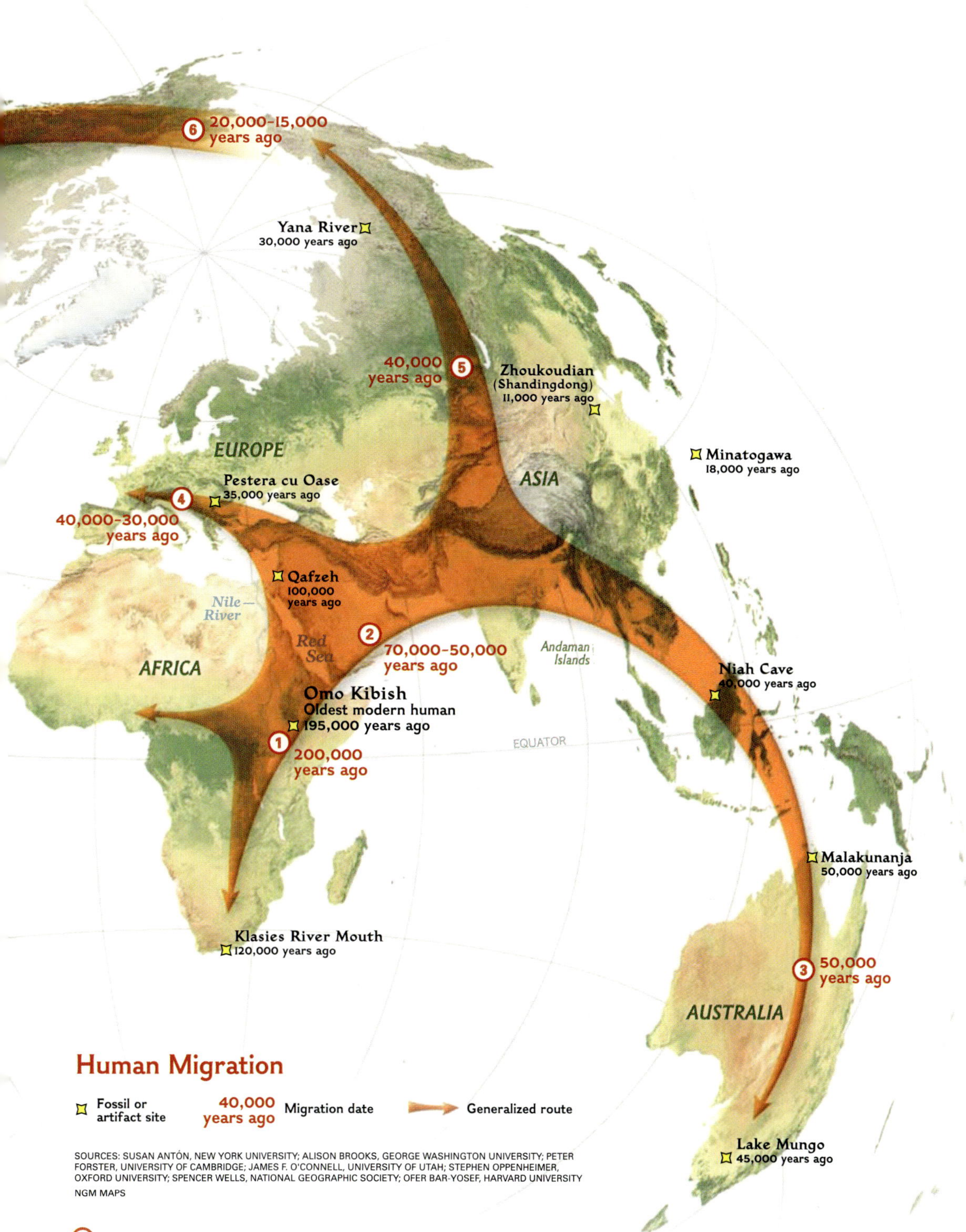

6 INTO THE NEW WORLD

Exactly when the first people arrived in the Americas is still hotly debated. Genetic evidence suggests it was between 20,000 and 15,000 years ago, when sea levels were low and land connected Siberia to Alaska. Ice sheets would have covered the interior of North America, forcing the new arrivals to travel down the west coast.

PHOTO BY KENNETH GARRETT

History on a Chromosome

Genetic mutations act as markers, tracing a journey through time. The earliest known mutation to spread outside Africa is M168, which arose some 50,000 years ago. This graphic shows the Y chromosome of a Native American man with various mutations including M168, proving his African ancestry.

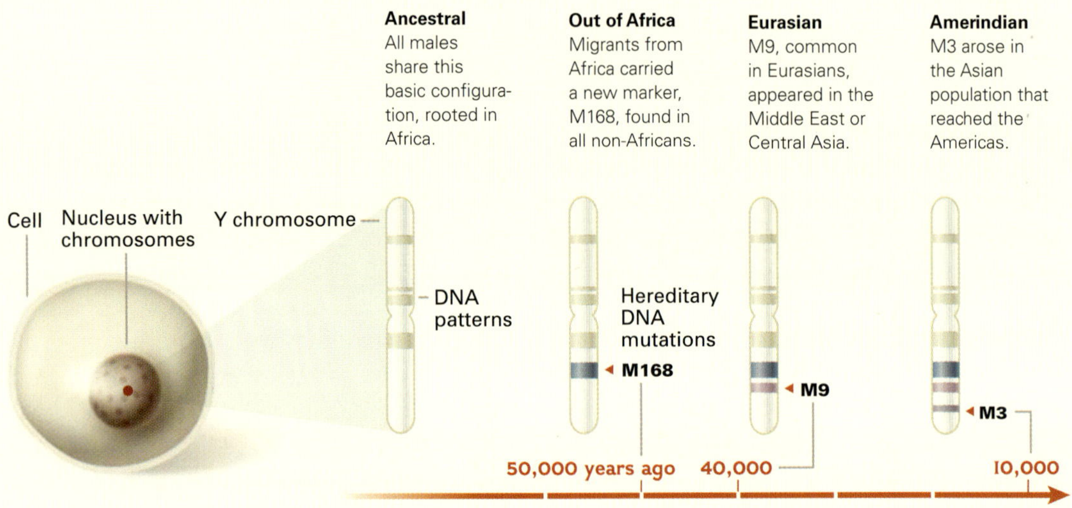

(Continued from page 7) doomed caretaker of a continent—would have interacted is a potent mystery. Did they eye each other with wonder or in fear? Did they fight, socialize, or dismiss each other as alien beings?

All we know is that as modern humans and distinctly more sophisticated toolmaking spread into Europe, the once ubiquitous Neandertals were squeezed into ever shrinking pockets of habitation that eventually petered out completely. On current evidence, the two groups interbred rarely, if at all. Neither mtDNA from Neandertal fossils nor modern human DNA bears any trace of an ancient mingling of the bloodlines.

About the same time as modern humans pushed into Europe, some of the same group that had paused in the Middle East spread east into Central Asia. Following herds of game, skirting mountain ranges and deserts, they reached southern Siberia as early as 40,000 years ago. As populations diverged and became isolated, their genetic lineages likewise branched and rebranched. But the isolation was rarely if ever complete. "People have always met other people, found them attractive, and had children," says molecular anthropologist Theodore Schurr of the University of Pennsylvania.

Schurr's specialty is the peopling of the Americas—one of the last and most contentious chapters in the human story. The subject seems to attract fantastic theories (Native Americans are the descendants of the ancient Israelites or the lost civilization of Atlantis) as well as ones tinged with a political agenda. The "Caucasoid" features of a 9,500-year-old skull from Washington State called Kennewick Man, for instance, have been hailed as proof that the first Americans came from northern Europe.

DNA studies have confirmed this opening chapter of our story over and over: All the variously shaped and shaded people of Earth trace their ancestry to African hunter-gatherers, some 150,000 years ago.

In fact most scientists agree that today's Native Americans descend from ancient Asians who crossed from Siberia to Alaska in the last ice age, when low sea level would have exposed a land bridge between the continents. But there's plenty of debate about when they came and where they originated in Asia.

For decades the first Americans were thought to have arrived around 13,000 years ago as the Ice Age eased, opening a path through the ice covering Canada. But a few archaeologists claimed to have evidence for an earlier arrival, and two early sites withstood repeated criticism: the Meadow-croft Shelter in Pennsylvania, now believed to be about 16,000 years old, and Monte Verde in southern Chile, more than 14,000 years old.

The DNA of living Native Americans can help settle some of the disputes. Most carry markers that link them unequivocally to Asia. The same markers cluster in people who today inhabit the Altay region of southern Siberia, suggesting it was the starting point for a journey across the land bridge. So far, the genetic evidence doesn't show whether North and South America were populated in a single, early migration or two or three distinct waves, and it suggests only a rough range of dates, between 20,000 and 15,000 years ago.

Even the youngest of those dates is older than the opening of an inland route through the Canadian ice. So how did the first Americans get here? They probably traveled along the coast: perhaps a few hundred people hopping from one pocket of land and sustenance to the next, between a frigid ocean and a looming wall of ice. "A coastal route would have been the easiest way in," says Wells. "But it still would have been a hell of a trip."

Beyond the glaciers lay immense herds of bison, mammoths, and other animals on a continent innocent of other intelligent predators. Pushed by population growth or pulled by the lure of game, people spread to the tip of South America in as little as a thousand years.

The genes of today's Native Americans are helping to bring their ancestors' saga to life. But much of the story can only be imagined, says Jody Hey, a population geneticist at Rutgers University. "You can't tell it with the richness of what must have happened."

With the settling of the Americas, modern humans had conquered most of the planet. When European explorers set sail 700 years ago, the lands they "discovered" were already full of people. The encounters were often wary or violent, but they were the reunions of a close-knit family.

Perhaps the most wonderful of the stories hidden in our genes is that, when unraveled, the tangled knot of our global genetic diversity today leads us all back to a recent yesterday, together in Africa.

"The story of our ancestors is written in the simple DNA code of A, C, G, and T," says Spencer Wells, head of the National Geographic Society's Genographic Project. It will analyze DNA from hundreds of thousands of people to map how prehistoric humans populated the planet.

© 2006 MARK THIESSEN/National Geographic Image Collection.

A WORLD OF UNANSWERED QUESTIONS

While science has traced the outlines of human migrations, key questions remain, some of which appear below. The Genographic Project hopes to answer many of them with help from geneticists at 11 centers worldwide, who will draw DNA from blood and cheek swabs of living people and extract it from fossils. By comparing lineages, they hope to piece together the scattered puzzle of the human journey.

Sub-Saharan Africa

Fundamental riddles in the land where the human story began

At the National Health Laboratory Service in Johannesburg, South Africa, Himla Soodyall will try to find out which African populations harbor the most ancient genetic lineages and map patterns of diversity within sub-Saharan Africa. She'll also explore the impact of migrations into Africa.

North Africa/Middle East

Did Alexander the Great and the Romans leave a genetic trail?

Pierre A. Zalloua of the American University of Beirut Medical Center will explore the genetic legacy of ancient armies and empires. He will also try to identify the earliest inhabitants of the Sahara.

South Asia

The complicated branches of India's genetic tree

At Madurai Kamaraj University in Tamil Nadu, India, Ramasamy Pitchappan will try to understand what role the Indian caste system has had in determining genetic patterns, and if there was an influx of Indo-European language speakers from Central Asia 3,500 years ago.

East/Southeast Asia

Hopping islands and continents, and maybe the largest ocean

Li Jin of Fudan University in Shanghai, China, asks: When did people first reach Taiwan and Japan? What led to the north-south genetic divide among native populations in East Asia? Did ancient seafarers cross the Pacific from Asia to South America, and if so, where did they embark?

Australasia/Pacific Ocean

Following migratory tracks into the vast down under

John Mitchell of La Trobe University in Melbourne, Australia,

READING SECRETS OF THE BLOOD

In 1675 a bloody conflict broke out in New England between English colonists and the Wampanoag Indians. Led by their chief, Metacomet—known to the English as King Philip—the Wampanoag gathered other tribes to their side, but were ultimately no match for the firepower of the English. King Philip's War ended a year later, with Philip's severed head displayed on a pole in Plymouth and virtually all of his people killed or forced into servitude. For the next 300 years, their descendants lived and died on the fringes of society while modern New England rose up around them.

On a warm late summer evening last year, a few dozen people from today's Wampanoag Nation gathered in the American Legion Hall in Seekonk, Massachusetts. Except for a few Native Pride baseball caps and some Indian jewelry, they looked like a cross section of working-class America—white, black, and brown, some young, some elderly—the kind of folk you might see at Fenway Park on a Sunday afternoon. But this wasn't a casual get-together. These members of the Seaconke-Wampanoag Tribe had come to give their blood to the Genographic Project, a global inquiry into humanity's deep collective past that could also shine a light on their own history.

Launched by the National Geographic Society with major support from the IBM Corporation and the Waitt Family Foundation, the project hopes to use genetic information gleaned from a thousand indigenous populations around the world to enhance wants to learn when and how the first modern humans reached Australia and Papua New Guinea—an event now generally thought to predate the arrival of the first modern humans in Europe. Also, how did the ancestors of the Maori reach New Zealand?

North Eurasia

Staging ground for migrations to Europe and the Americas

Elena Balanovska of the Research Centre for Medical Genetics in Moscow, Russia, will study the enigma of the Caucasus Mountains: Were they a bridge or a barrier between Europe and Asia? What is the link between the high degrees of linguistic and genetic diversity in the region? She will also search for clues about who first settled Siberia and which groups continued on to the Americas.

Central/Western Europe

The legacy of hunter-gatherers, farmers, and empires

At two institutes—France's Institut Pasteur in Paris and the United Kingdom's Wellcome Trust Sanger Institute in Cambridge—Lluis Quintana-Murci and Chris Tyler-Smith are examining mitochondrial DNA and the Y chromosome, respectively, for traces of ancient European hunter-gatherers and early farmers. They will also study whether great European empires have left detectable genetic marks. And are the Basque people as distinct from their neighbors as their unique language suggests?

North America

How Native Asians became the Native Americans of today

Theodore Schurr at the University of Pennsylvania in Philadelphia will weigh in on controversial questions: When did people first reach the New World, and what routes did they follow from Asia?

South America

The end of the road for wanderers from Asia

At Brazil's Universidade Federal de Minas Gerais, Fabricio R. Santos is asking: When did people first arrive in South America, and are their descendants still alive today? Did the indigenous people of the Andes originate in the Amazon?

Ancient DNA

If fossil genes could speak, what might they tell us?

A lab run by Alan Cooper of the Australian Centre for Ancient DNA will study human remains. DNA from old teeth and bones could show when the genetic markers seen today first appeared and help scientists test their picture of ancient migrations.

our understanding of humanity's ancient migrations around the planet. Conceived and directed by National Geographic Explorer-in-Residence Spencer Wells, it is among the most ambitious and potentially most informative projects the Society has ever undertaken. It may also prove to be one of the more controversial.

The Seaconke-Wampanoag were the first U.S. group to participate. As more people trickled into the Legion Hall, University of Pennsylvania molecular anthropologist Theodore Schurr and a colleague set up a makeshift blood collection station. Schurr is coordinating Genographic research in North America, and over the project's five-year scope, he and his team intend to analyze DNA from up to a hundred indigenous groups. The resulting flood of data could help resolve long-standing debates about how, when, and from where the Americas were first populated.

Other investigators will try to pin down details of migrations across the rest of the globe. But the project's success depends on the willingness of indigenous groups here and abroad to volunteer. More than a dozen have already signed up, from the Caucasus Mountains to Laos, and hundreds more will be needed. "If this works for us, we're hoping other tribes will jump in and give their DNA too," says Seaconke-Wampanoag Chief George Silver Wolf Jennings.

In the early 1990s the pioneering population geneticist Luca Cavalli-Sforza of Stanford University and his colleagues conceived the Human Genome Diversity Project (HGDP) with similar goals in mind. But the plan ran into heated opposition. Some indigenous groups bridled at the notion that their DNA might be used to tell a story of their origins in conflict with their own traditional beliefs. Others balked at volunteering what they perceived might be patentable medical information and getting nothing in return. Still others found the project's intention to create self-propagating cell lines from their blood disturbing, even sacrilegious. Amid the misunderstanding and protest, the HGDP never received the funding it needed.

Wells and his colleagues are taking pains to distinguish their effort from the HGDP. The Genographic Project will produce no cell lines or medically relevant data. It will also provide something tangible to indigenous groups, at the same time attracting new participants and gleaning some extra scientific data. For a fee, anyone can submit a cheek swab of DNA by mail, then learn about their own "deep ancestry." Proceeds will support research and go to educational and cultural preservation projects for indigenous groups.

So far, more than 100,000 cheek-swab kits have been sold, bringing in over 2.2 million dollars. The kits only reveal a small fraction of a person's full genetic ancestry, and some critics think the program raises unrealistic expectations. They also warn that distributing the money fairly will not be easy.

Wells has failed to win over some doubters. "The project inherently conflicts with indigenous interests," says Debra Harry of the Indigenous Peoples Council on Biocolonialism, an advocacy group that has called for a boycott of the National Geographic Society, IBM, and Gateway Computers, the source of funding for the Waitt Foundation. "The fundamental question the project is asking is 'Where do we come from?' That's not a question that is of interest to us as indigenous people. We already know where we came from."

"If people feel strongly, they don't have to participate," says Wells. "But we find that most people are excited to learn that they carry a record of their ancestry in their blood." Michael Tender Heart Markley, chairperson of the Seaconke-Wampanoag, agrees. "Because the project uses our genetics to track our path, it is really us, the Seaconke-Wampanoag Tribe, telling our own story."

The tribe's DNA is unlikely to yield any simple truths, at least in the short term. Native American groups like the Seaconke-Wampanoag have European and African as well as Native American ancestry. And as Theodore Schurr explains to those donating blood, the initial results won't reveal a person's full heritage. They could point back to Metacomet's people—or to ancestors from another continent.

A fuller picture will emerge only after the project analyzes each person's full set of chromosomes and compares them with the Genographic Project's growing lode of DNA from other groups.

Says Chief Jennings: "I just hope these guys aren't gonna tell us we're all Swedish."

Discussion Questions

- What types of information can geneticists derive from mutations, mtDNA and Y chromosomes? What are their limitations?
- How might fossil evidence and genetics complement each other in tracing ancient migrations? What advantages and disadvantages does one line of evidence have over the other?
- According to this article, what fossil, genographic, and linguistic evidence are used to support the Out-of-Africa theory in reference to Modern Humans?
- What are some of the arguments in opposition to human genomic undertakings?

Join the Debate

Visit http://news.stanford.edu/pr/93/930608Arc3222.html for Stanford's 1993 news release concerning the ethical issues involved with the Human Genome Diversity Project.

- What are some of the ethical issues involved?
- What is your stance on the arguments for and against the endeavors of the HGDP?
- How important is the "origins story" to you and how far back would you care to trace your ancestry?
- How would you address the popular question: Who owns the human genome?

Next, browse the web for indigenous groups and councils against the human genome project.

- How do the ethical issues posed by indigenous groups compare and differ to those raised in the 1993 Stanford news release?

Field Journal: Mitochondrial Eve and Y-Chromosomal Adam

This article references mtDNA (genealogically known as the Mitochondrial Eve) passed down from mothers to her offspring, and the Y-chromosome (Y-Chromosomal Adam) passed down from fathers to their sons.[1] The study of molecular evolution and tracing genetic markers back to common ancestors rely on mutations of mtDNA and the Y-chromosome.

- Familiarize yourself with the basic concepts of molecular genealogy, particularly mtDNA, Y-chromosome, mutation, and haplotypes (short video clips are are available at http://learn.genetics.utah.edu/content/extras/molgen/).
- Look up the haplogroups associated with Mitochondrial Eve and the haplogroups of Y-Chromosomal Adam, and look up the areas of the world to which they can be traced.

What possible haplogroups can be found in your genetic makeup? To what regions of the world might that connect you?

---

[1]*A For an overview and more detailed information on genetics, genealogy, mutations, and haplotypes, explore Learn.Genetics of the Genetic Science Learning Center at the University of Utah, specifically "Heredity & Traits" and "Molecular Genealogy."*

ALMOST HUMAN

Anthropologist Jill Pruetz's study of the Fongoli chimps reveals a sub-culture of behaviors that ultimately shift traditional paradigms of both chimp and early-human ecological intelligence. Pruetz's observations, among them of the hotly debated bush-baby spearing technology and the prominent role of female chimps in hunting and tool use, necessarily blur and complicate the boundary between humans and chimps—in essence, what it means to be human.

As you read "Almost Human," consider the following questions:

- How do environmental factors influence primate adaptive behavior and technology?
- In what ways do the Fongoli chimps reinforce or alter traditional knowledge of chimpanzees?
- How does our view of chimpanzees affect human/chimp relations?
- What insights can Pruetz's study provide into the evolutionary story of our hominid ancestors?

An adult male lingers at Sakoto pool, a favorite spot among the community of chimps scientists call the Fongoli group, for a stream that runs through their range.

ALMOST HUMAN

By Mary Roach

Photographs by Frans Lanting

First-time mom Nickel reclines with her newborn, Teva, one of the newest members of the chimp group being studied at Fongoli. All the chimps clamored to groom the baby, but Nickel let Mike, an orphan, get close. She avoided adult males, prone to noisy fits of branch shaking.

ON THE SAVANNAS OF SENEGAL, CHIMPANZEES ARE HUNTING BUSH BABIES WITH SPEARLIKE STICKS.

THIS HOTHOUSE OF CHIMP "TECHNOLOGY"

OFFERS CLUES TO OUR OWN EVOLUTION.

Chimps that live on the ground, rather than in the safety of treetops, tend to be wary of large strangers.

Daybreak is sudden and swift, as though an unseen hand had simply reached out and raised a dimmer switch. Cued by the dawn, thirty-four chimpanzees awaken.

They are still in the nests they built the previous night, in trees at the edge of an open plateau.

A wild chimpanzee does not get out of bed quietly. Chimps wake up hollering. There are technical names for what I'm hearing—pant-hoots, pant-barks, screams, hoos—but to a newcomer's ear, it's just a crazy, exuberant, escalating racket. You can't listen without grinning.

These are not chimps you've seen in these pages before. They're savanna-woodland chimps, found in eastern Senegal and across the border in western Mali. Unlike their better-known rain forest kin, savanna-woodland chimps spend most of their day on the ground. There is no canopy here. The trees are low and grow sparsely. It's an environment very much like the open, scratchy terrain where early humans evolved. For this reason, chimpanzee communities like the Fongoli group—named for a stream that runs through its range—are uniquely valuable to scientists who study the origins of our species.

By 8 a.m. my chintzy key-chain thermometer says it's 90 degrees. Our shirts are marked by the same white salt lines that appear on people's boots in winter. Here it's salt from sweat. The plateau we're crossing is a terrain of nothing, of red rocks and skin cancer, with no trees to break the fall of equatorial sun. In our backpacks we each carry three liters of water. It was cool when we set out. By noon it will be hot enough to steep tea.

I'm not complaining. I'm making a point. Life on the savanna—even so-called mosaic savanna, tempered by patches of lusher gallery forest along the streambeds—is exceptionally harsh. If you are a primate used to greener terrain, you must adjust your behavior to survive. Our earliest hominin (meaning bipedal ape) ancestors evolved more than five million years ago during the Miocene, an epoch of extreme drying that saw the creation of vast tracts of grassland. Tropical *(Continued on page 24)*

Adapted from "Almost Human" by Mary Roach: National Geographic Magazine, April 2008.

Savanna-woodland chimps, unlike their rain forest brethren, spend most of their waking time on the ground searching for food and water. Fongoli's mix of grassland, low trees, and a hot dry season mirrors the environment that eventually propelled early humans to hunt and use tools.

(Continued from page 21) primates on the perimeter of their range no longer had plentiful fruits and year-round streams and lakes. They were forced to adapt, to range farther in their search for food and water, to take advantage of other resources. In short, to get creative.

The media ruckus spurred by Pruetz's report of spear-wielding chimps made her absence as a speaker at last year's Mind of the Chimpanzee conference perplexing.

In 2007 Jill Pruetz, an anthropologist at Iowa State University, reported that a Fongoli female chimp named Tumbo was seen two years earlier, less than a mile from where we are right now, sharpening a branch with her teeth and wielding it like a spear. She used it to stab at a bush baby—a pocket-size, tree-dwelling nocturnal primate that springs from branch to branch like a grasshopper. Until that report, the regular making of tools for hunting and killing mammals had been considered uniquely human behavior. Over a span of 17 days at the start of the 2006 rainy season, Pruetz saw the chimps hunt bush babies 13 times. There were 18 sightings in 2007. It would appear the chimps are getting creative.

There are individuals who are uncomfortable with Pruetz's tales of spear-wielding chimps, and not all of them are bush babies. Harvard professor of biological anthropology Richard Wrangham, who has studied chimpanzee aggression in Uganda's Kibale National Park, has been skeptical. Wrangham is widely known for his "demonic male" theory, which holds that the savage murders carried out by male chimps while policing their turf are suggestive of a violent nature at the core of man. Primatologist Craig Stanford, author of The Hunting Apes, also downplays the importance of Pruetz's findings. "This behavior is fascinating, but the observations are so preliminary that it merits only a short note in a journal."

The report ran in the major journal Current Biology, and people seemed to find it interesting. In the week that followed, Pruetz's findings were featured in more than 300 news and science outlets, including New Scientist, the New York Times, the Washington Post, and NPR's Science Friday. The Smithsonian Institution requested one of the spears. In short, it was the most widely talked about primatology news since the reports of infanticide and cannibalism at Jane Goodall's site at Gombe in the 1970s.

Pruetz and I watch the chimps climb from their nests. A large male hangs from a low branch by one arm, swinging gently, in no hurry. The silhouette is utterly erect, arrestingly humanoid. He lets go, drops to the ground, and moves off across the plateau. The symbolism is impossible to miss. Here is a chimpanzee, thought by many to be the closest thing we have to a living model of our early hominin ancestors, literally dropping from the trees and moving out into the open expanses of the savanna. It is as though we are watching time-lapse footage of human evolution, the dawn of man unfolding in our binoculars.

Jill Pruetz spent four years getting the Fongoli chimpanzees accustomed to the presence of humans—what primatologists call habituating them—and the past three summers observing them. Six days a week, from dawn to dusk, she follows the chimps.

It is not glamorous work. It's hot and filthy and exhausting. Home is a mud-walled hut and a drop toilet shared with 30 Fongoli villagers. Dinner is peanut sauce over rice, except when it's peanut sauce over millet. If the chimps wander unusually far, Pruetz gets back to the village so late that her portion has long ago been fed to the dogs. Sometimes, rather than hike the five miles back to camp, she curls up and sleeps on the ground (or takes a nap in an abandoned chimp nest). She has gotten malaria seven times.

Yet you rarely meet people who love what they do as much as Pruetz does. Right now she is sitting on the *(Continued on page 28)*

Plotting his move? Lupin, a large teenage male, seems to have alpha ambitions, but chimp politics require more than brute strength—winning friends is critical.

Primatologist Jill Pruetz holds one of the first known "spears" used by a chimp. She made headlines with her report of chimps hunting bush babies by jamming modified sticks into tree-hole burrows (right). The technique appears to be used most often by females and the young, which may engineer new foraging methods when food is scarce and males refuse to share.

(Continued from page 24) ground, jotting notes with one hand and slapping sweat bees with the other. Blood from a blister has soaked through the heel of her sock. To listen to Pruetz, we might as well be in Paris. "Sometimes," she says, scratching a bite, "I think I'm going to wake up and it's all a dream." The payoffs have been dramatic. In addition to using tools to hunt, Fongoli chimps have been exhibiting some other novel behaviors: soaking in a water hole, passing the afternoon in caves.

At 24 square miles, Fongoli is the largest home range of any habituated chimpanzee group ever studied. (Jane Goodall's Gombe chimps, by comparison, roam over five square miles.) Craig Stanford likens foraging over a large range to knowing one's way around an enormous supermarket. Like Pruetz, he believes the chimpanzees are not foraging at random, but moving with foresight and intent. "You don't stroll down the aisles hoping to catch a glimpse of the broccoli. You know where each item is, and in which months seasonal foods are likely to be in stock." The same, he thinks, holds true for chimpanzees.

"Ecological intelligence" is the name of the theory that some primates, including those of our lineage, have evolved larger, more complex brains because it helped them adapt to the challenges of surviving in a less giving habitat. "The first push toward a larger brain," writes Stanford, "may have been the result of a patchily distributed, high-quality diet and the cognitive mapping capabilities that accompanied it."

High-quality, meaning: meat. The shift toward eating more meat may have played an important role in the evolution of a larger, more sophisticated brain. Here's how the thinking goes. Brains are, to use terminology coined by researchers Leslie Aiello and Peter Wheeler, "expensive tissue." To keep a bigger brain functioning, some other organ or system needed to become more streamlined. A chimp doesn't have to eat nearly as much of an energy-rich food like meat as he would of low-nutrient plant matter. Expending less energy on digestion means you can afford to apply it elsewhere, perhaps to power an expanded brain.

As if on cue, a female named Tia appears in our sight lines 20 feet ahead, sitting on a boulder pulling raw flesh off a limb like a picnicker with a comically huge drumstick. Pruetz raises her binoculars, then lowers them again. "Holy crap! It's a bushbuck." She can tell from the white markings on the hide, a long strip of which hangs from the leg. "That's the biggest animal I've seen them eat." She surmises it was a fawn. Gombe chimps have occasionally killed bushbuck fawns as well. They are the largest prey on record for a chimpanzee.

Hunting at Fongoli coincides with the rainy season, and Pruetz has some theories about why this is. As water holes fill and shoots and other greenery become more plentiful with the rain, the land provides enough sustenance to support a sizable group of chimps on the move. There are advantages to traveling in a large group. A single chimp or small group that heads out on its own can easily lose track of the community for days at a time. For a chimp, sociability is important. Pruetz points to an estrous female named Sissy, her pink swelling bobbing behind her like a bustle. "Otherwise you miss out on that." She means, of course, the chance to mate, to pass along your genetic material.

Right now, two rains into the rainy season, there's enough water and food for the group to travel together, but just barely. Pruetz believes it is this scenario—large crowd competing for limited resources—that has pushed certain members of the community to try their hand at novel things.

Things like sharpening sticks to spear bush babies. It is a different kind of hunting than the organized colobus monkey raids documented at other sites. A chimp who comes across a dead, hollow tree limb—promising real estate for day-sleeping bush babies—will sometimes break off a branch from a nearby tree, remove the leaves and the flimsy ends, and then use its teeth to whittle one end to a point. This tool is then stabbed into an opening in the tree limb until the animal inside is out of commission. Whereupon it is eaten, head first, Pruetz says, "like a popsicle."

Adult female and juvenile chimps—the low rankers—have been seen hunting bush babies most often. This makes sense. Dominant males are not generous with food they find, and no one can force them to share. Fongoli females appear to have taken matters into their own hands.

The chimp named Sissy sits motionless and hunched at a low termite mound twenty feet from us.

Now here comes Farafa, her baby Fanta on her back and a bushbuck haunch in her jaws. It's a complicated, messy piece of anatomy, with sinew and hide hanging off one end. Tia sees her and stands up to move away. My last glimpse of Tia is with her now bare bone brandished above her head, standing erect, as though reenacting the "dawn of man" scene from *2001: A Space Odyssey.* Fongoli chimps have a flair for the dramatic.

She was in the audience but wasn't invited to present a paper. On top of that, Pruetz's post-doc adviser, Cambridge University primatologist William McGrew, made a passing reference to the Fongoli hunting behaviors but did not credit her with the work. He credited her co-author and former student Paco Bertolani, now a student of McGrew's. Bertolani witnessed the first—of now 40—observed instances of the behavior, but scientific etiquette would call for the principal investigator to be mentioned. McGrew apologized afterward. Some primatologists took Pruetz to task for overstating the bush-baby-spearing behavior. When your prey is smaller than your hand, are you really hunting? Male primatologists tend to make the distinction along gender lines: The traditional view has been that chimpanzee hunting—along with aggression and murder—is the domain of the male. "Small mammals that females and juveniles obtain are 'gathered,'" Pruetz says, "while males 'hunt.'" Females, the thinking goes, don't hunt because they don't need to; male chimps are thought by some to trade meat for sex, but Pruetz hasn't seen this at Fongoli.

I'm going to weigh in, for what it's worth. One day while accompanying Pruetz, I watched a young chimp named David at a bush baby tree hole. We heard him well before we saw him: a resounding THONK that caused Pruetz to stop in her tracks and go, "Hold on, hold the phone, that sounds like a spear!" We looked around, and there he was, standing on a branch in a kino tree, holding on with one hand and waving a thick, three-foot-long stick over his head. He slammed it down into the hole, then examined the tip. Concluding that no one was home, he took off, leaving the spear protruding from the hole. The violence and foresight with which he undertook his task did not suggest an animal quietly foraging. His aim was unmistakable: to kill, or at least incapacitate, whatever was in there.

Many of Pruetz's reviewers tripped over the word spear. For one thing, it suggests a projectile and a more Cro-Magnon-esque technique: something aimed and thrown. (Pruetz says she had spearfishing in mind when she chose the noun.) Stanford suggested bludgeon. But bludgeons are blunt, not sharpened. Another offered dagger. Someone else wanted bayonet. In the end, Pruetz took spear out of the title and worded her text more cautiously, making reference to a tool "used in the manner of a spear." (The press picked up on it anyway. "Spear-Wielding Chimps Snack on Skewered Bushbabies" ran the giddy NewScientist.com headline.)

I asked Pruetz if perhaps she's been the victim of an alpha male primatologist conspiracy. She laughed it off. "Yeah, maybe I'm not pant-grunting enough." (The pant-grunt is an expression of submissiveness; a chimp that encounters a higher ranked peer and fails to pant-grunt is asking for trouble.) It's also possible that humans are simply resistant to the notion that anyone other than a human makes weapons for killing.

You would think that primatologists, more than other scientists, would be comfortable with the shifting boundaries between chimpanzee and human. Their gene sequences are around 95 to 98 percent the *(Continued on page 34)*

CHIMP CULTURES

Just as humans use chopsticks in one culture and forks in another, scientists now realize that chimpanzees also develop different cultural practices depending on where they live. Chimpanzees in ten well-studied sub-Saharan communities have devised the following variations on common behaviors.

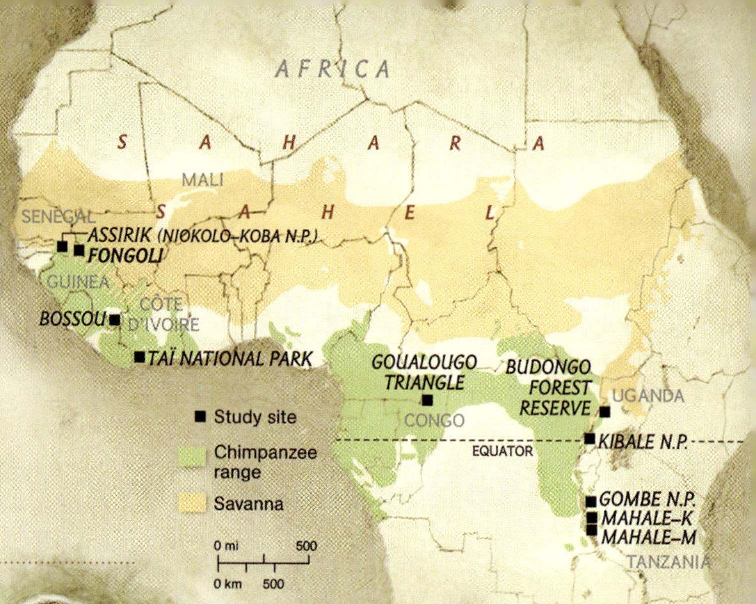

► Use of hammer and/or anvil

Chimps use rocks to smash open nuts and fruits for food.

WHERE
- Fongoli
- Assirik
- Bossou
- Gombe
- Taï

VARIATION
Taï chimps also use wood to crack nuts. Fongoli and Assirik chimps slam baobab fruit against rocks.

▼ Leaf sponge

Chimps chew leaves into spongy wads to soak up water for drinking.

WHERE
All sites except Mahale–K

VARIATION
Chimps in some groups poke leaf sponges into tree holes to absorb collected rainwater, while others dip their sponges into streams.

▲ Going into water

Chimps in most communities avoid major contact with water, but three groups enter streams or pools.

WHERE
- Fongoli
- Bossou
- Mahale–M

VARIATION
At Fongoli chimps sit in waist-high water or lie in shallow pools. Bossou chimps wade but don't sit down. Mahale chimps display by splashing.

▲ Termite fishing

Chimps often use twigs, grass, or vines to fish termites from mounds.

WHERE
- Fongoli
- Gombe
- Goualougo
- Mahale—K

VARIATION
Apes get larger helpings of termites at Fongoli and Goualougo by first fraying the end of their fishing tools to create more surface space to snag the bugs.

ART BY FERNANDO G. BAPTISTA, NG STAFF

MAP BY LISA R. RITTER, NG STAFF

CONSULTANT: ANDREW WHITEN, COLLABORATIVE CHIMPANZEE CULTURES PROJECT, UNIVERSITY OF ST. ANDREWS

CHIMPANZEE RANGE: THOMAS BUTYNSKI, CONSERVATION INTERNATIONAL; UNEP-WCMC

◀ Rain dance

A storm can provoke chimps in most groups to show off with a frenetic or rhythmic display.

WHERE
All sites (though unconfirmed at Assirik)

VARIATION
Before a storm Taï chimps perform a slow and often silent dance.

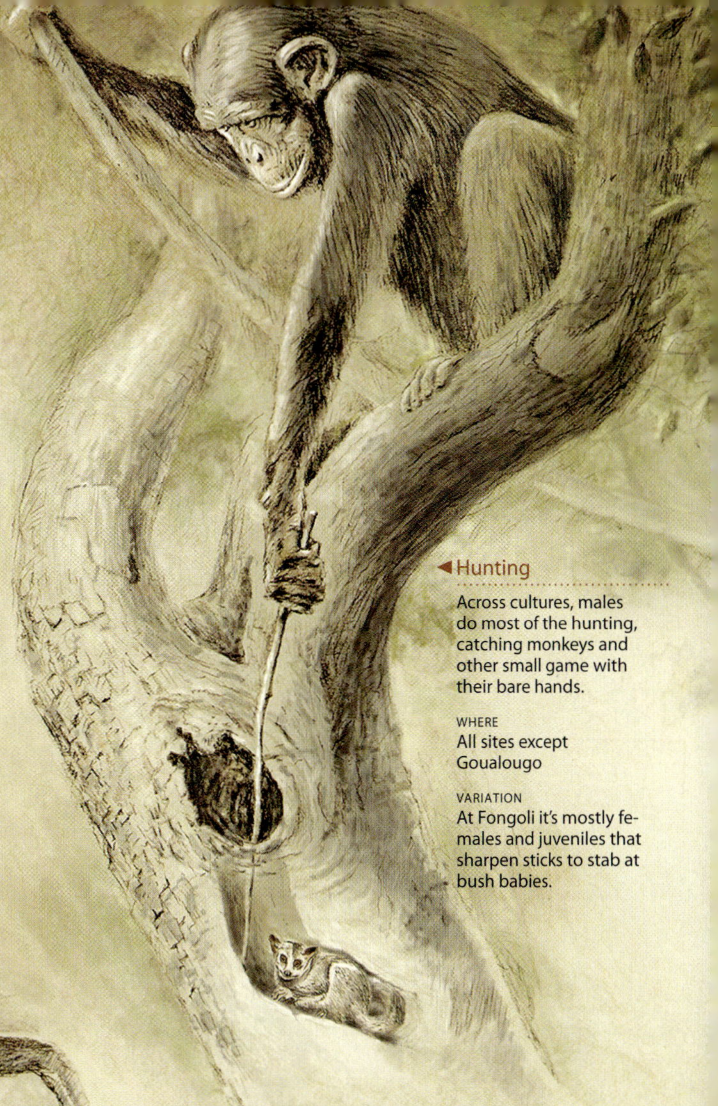

▼ Rock throwing

Rocks are hurled, sometimes as weapons and other times as part of a display.

WHERE
All sites except Budongo and Goualougo

VARIATION
Mahale males tend to throw rocks into water as part of their displays.

◀ Hunting

Across cultures, males do most of the hunting, catching monkeys and other small game with their bare hands.

WHERE
All sites except Goualougo

VARIATION
At Fongoli it's mostly females and juveniles that sharpen sticks to stab at bush babies.

▼ Leaf clipping

Chimps often bite off bits of leaves and spit them out to get each other's attention or show anxiety.

WHERE
•Fongoli
•Bossou
•Kibale
•Mahale–K
•Mahale–M
•Taï

VARIATION
Mahale chimps also clip leaves during courtship, while at Fongoli and Taï, males usually clip leaves before a display. Fongoli females do it when they have hiccups.

▼ A-frame grooming

Several groups hold hands over their heads while grooming.

WHERE
All sites except Bossou and Budongo

VARIATION
Mahale chimps grasp palms or wrists, with the dominant chimp's wrist on top. At Gombe they hold branches instead. Fongoli chimps use both customs.

The only infant born in the Fongoli group last spring, Teva is the first baby scientists were able to track within a week or two of her birth. Closely monitoring her development will provide valuable insights into how chimps pass on behaviors. "Her mother is one of the most prolific hunters," says Pruetz. "It will be interesting to see if Teva picks it up."

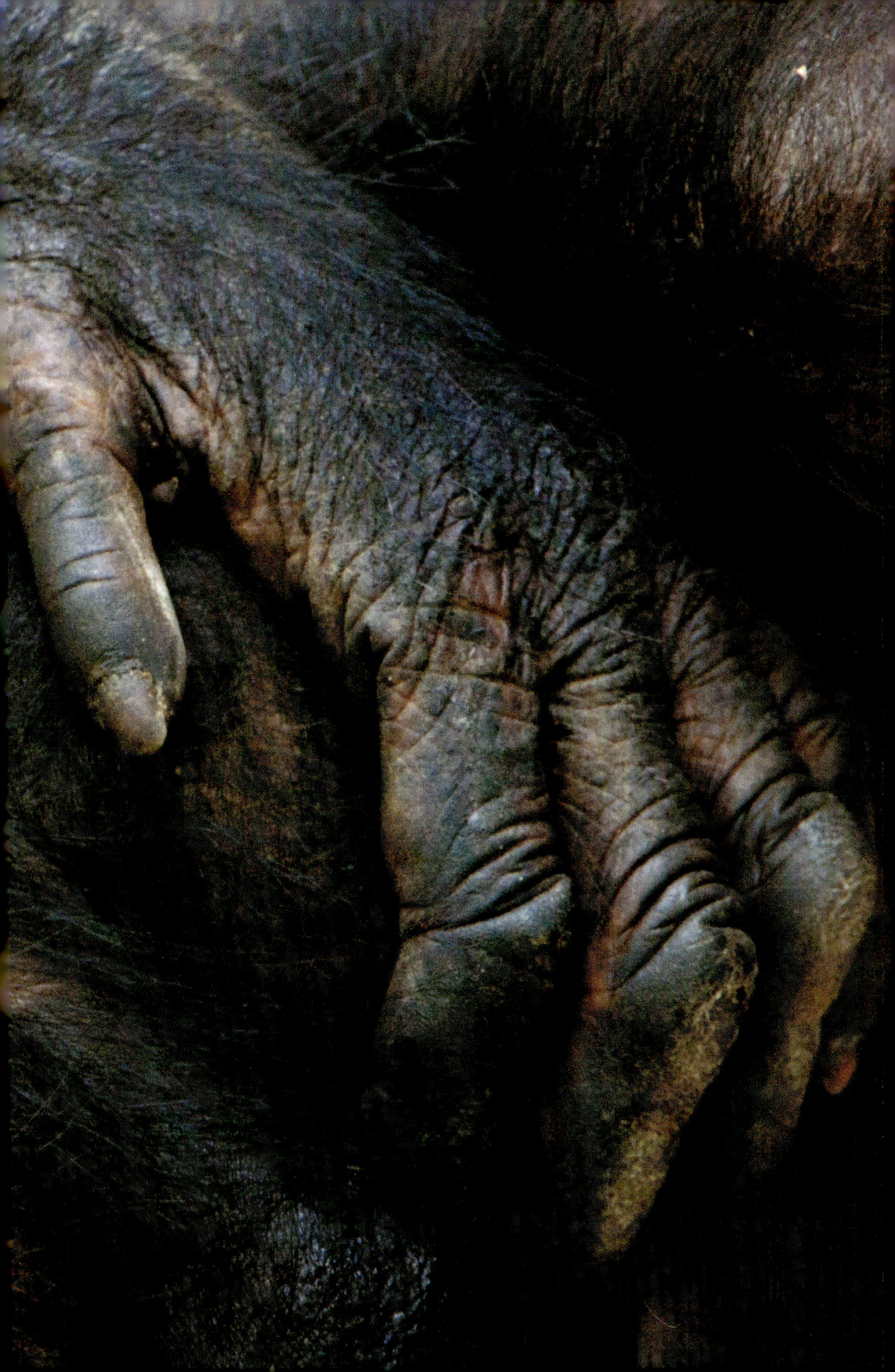

(Continued from page 29) same. (This is less meaningful than it sounds. Humans share more than 80 percent of their gene sequence with mice, and maybe 40 percent with lettuce.) A recent exploration of the human and chimpanzee genomes, undertaken by David Reich and colleagues at the Broad Institute of MIT and Harvard in Cambridge, Massachusetts, suggests that chimpanzees and early hominins may have interbred after the two lines initially split. Yet there seems to be a lingering discomfort with findings that, as Pruetz puts it, "chip away at our superiority."

Pruetz and I are sitting along a forested ravine where the chimps rest during the day's hottest hours.

Since the earliest days of primatology, discoveries of chimp behavior that threaten to undermine the specialness—the apartness—of human beings have met with rancorous resistance. Many anthropologists bristled at the first references to chimpanzee "culture"—a concept widely accepted today. Jane Goodall's first reports of chimps making tools (for termite fishing) were as contentious in their day as more recent claims of teaching chimps to use language. At the Great Ape Trust, in Des Moines, Iowa, a bonobo named Kanzi has learned to communicate through symbols. Kanzi commands about 380 symbols and shows signs of understanding their meaning. When he was frightened by a beaver, an animal for which he had no symbol, he selected the symbols for "water" and "gorilla" (an animal that scares him). Critics say the communications are purely conditioned behavior. Novel uses of symbols—e.g., "water gorilla"—are dismissed as coincidence.

An exception to these attitudes has long been found at the Primate Research Institute at Kyoto University. Japanese primatology is consistent with the Buddhist precept that humans are a part of the natural world, not above or separate from it. At the Mind of the Chimpanzee conference in Chicago last year, Tetsuro Matsuzawa spoke of primatology's early years, when scientists "didn't know how much close we are." He added, with unabashed awe: "So close, like horse and zebra." In the background of one Japanese researcher's slides was what looked to be a chimp wearing glasses. I turned to the man next to me. "I'm sorry," I said. "I must be losing my mind. Was that chimp wearing glasses?" The man told me the Japanese primatologists had noticed the chimp was nearsighted and had him outfitted with prescription lenses. (I later learned he was wrong: This chimp was just playing with the glasses. There once was a research chimp whose caretakers ordered her glasses, but that was in the U.S., not Japan.)

No one around Fongoli is sending chimps to the optician, but the animals are accorded a remarkable amount of respect by locals. Kerri Clavette, Pruetz's intern, interviewed villagers about their beliefs regarding chimpanzees and whether they hunted them. Among the region's main tribes—the Malinke, Bedik, Bassari, and Jahanka—chimps, compared with monkeys, have an elevated, almost human status. "Chimpanzees came from man, as they have similar hearts," a villager told Clavette. Behaviors normally associated with a baser nature—such as walking on all fours—were given a respectful spin: "Chimpanzees walk on their knuckles to keep their hands clean to eat with." Chimpanzee origin myths feature humans running off into the woods for some reason—war, fear of circumcision, fear of being punished for fishing on Saturday—and staying there so long that they turn into chimpanzees.

Despite a local history of killing chimpanzees for medicinal reasons—the meat laid on a person's arm or eaten for strength, the brains prepared with couscous to treat mental illness—villagers rarely hunt chimpanzees in eastern Senegal today. Sadly, the taboo against eating one's almost kin has broken down in central Africa, where turmoil has worsened dire economic circumstances and chimps are sold as bush meat.

Attitudes in the West have been shifting gradually over the past few decades. The sequencing of the chimp genome, completed in 2005, has focused attention anew. New Zealand, the Netherlands, Sweden, and the United Kingdom have all passed legislation limiting experimentation on great apes, and the Balearic Islands in Spain passed a resolution in 2007 granting them basic legal rights. In 2006 an Austrian animal rights organization submitted an application to a district court in Mödling to appoint a legal guardian for a chimp named Hiasl. The strategy was to establish "legal person" status for the hairy defendant. (The judge was sympathetic but refused.) It is perhaps less problematic to view the situation as does The Third Chimpanzee author Jared Diamond: not that chimps are a kind of human, but that humans are a kind of chimp.

Only her right arm moves, pushing a saba vine probe into a hole and gently withdrawing it, with termites clinging to it. She raises it carefully to her mouth like a pensioner spooning soup. The mound is across an open lay of pebbly, brick-colored laterite that gives the ground the look of a clay tennis court.

Like fly-fishing, termite fishing is a meditative, deceptively nuanced activity. I tried it a few times and could not even find an active hole. My probe never sinks farther than an inch or so; the chimps regularly bury theirs a foot or more. They can find active holes by smell, inserting a probe and then sniffing the end of it for the smell of soldier termite pheromone.

Fongoli chimps eat termites year-round, not just in the dry season, when other foods are scarce. Termites make up, at bare minimum, 6 percent of the Fongoli chimps' diet. We know this because most evenings at six o'clock research assistant Sally Macdonald sits down with a set of sieves and buckets, and one or two ziplock bags of the chimp feces that the researchers bring back most days. She scans the fruit seeds, estimates the percentage of fiber from leaves and shoots, and takes note of bones and termite pincers. "Science in all its glamour," deadpans Macdonald, whose mother sends ziplock bags but does not know their fate.

A quick glimpse into the bucket reveals that saba fruit is the chimps' mainstay this time of year, an adult averaging 30 to 40 a day. The Fongoli record for saba seeds in a single fecal sample—499, compared with an average of 75—probably belongs to a male named Mamadou. Which may explain why Mamadou is, quoting Pruetz, "especially gassy."

Pruetz's Ph.D. student Stephanie Bogart says part of the reason chimps fish termites is that they're an exceptionally calorific food. A 3.5-ounce serving of termites has 613 calories, compared with chicken's 166. But 3.5 ounces of soldier termites is hundreds of insects, fished piecemeal from a mound. It's like eating cake one crumb at a time. The chimps must really like them.

Sissy gets up from her spot at the termite mound to select a new tool. She breaks off a length of vine, inspects it. Satisfied, she sticks it in her mouth and carries it back to the mound like a seamstress holding pins between her lips. Pruetz and others argue that female chimps are not only more skilled than males at crafting and using tools, but also more diligent. Craig Stanford agrees that it might well have been our female ancestors who first steered the culture toward tool use. Early tools for foraging, he imagines, gave way to tools for scavenging meat from carcasses killed and abandoned by large carnivores. These tools in turn may have paved the way for implements for killing prey. Which makes Pruetz's observations of chimps sharpening sticks and using them to whack bush babies all the more arresting: Fongoli's females seem to have skipped ahead to the killing tools. Barbecue tongs can't be all that far behind.

The vegetation is thicker here. We watch a slender green vine snake move through the grass. Birds are calling over our heads. One says cheerio; one actually says tweet. A third says whoop whoop whoop whoop whoop, like Curly of the Three Stooges. (When I ask what that one is, Pruetz replies, not at all sarcastically: "a bird." She is a woman of singular interests.)

Pruetz directs my gaze to a tangle of saba vines. Where I see a dark *(Continued on page 40)*

Most chimps avoid getting in water, but Fongoli males seek out pools to escape the 110-degree heat. "Pools are like the North Star for finding the chimps," says Pruetz. "They use them as a base and radiate out from them when they forage." The pile of rocks at right hides a camera.

Nellie, a young female, grips a limb with her feet as she tightropes some 30 feet above the forest floor. Chimps feature curved toe bones (right) that help them grasp trees and vines as they navigate the forest canopy. Observing apes walking on branches has led some scientists to speculate that bipedalism may have actually arisen in trees rather than on the ground.

(Continued from page 35) mass, she is able to distinguish six animals. The woman has chimp vision. (It's a condition that lingers long after she gets back to Iowa. "I get home and I'm looking for chimps on campus.") The animals can be so well hidden and so quiet that even Pruetz has trouble finding them. She sometimes locates them by smell—"chimp" being a potent variant of B.O. "Yesterday I thought I smelled chimp," Pruetz says, "but it was me."

> **Yet it is impossible to spend any time with chimpanzees and not be struck by how similar they are to us.**

The scene in the vines is one of drowsy, familial contentment. Yopogon is grooming Mamadou. Siberut is leaning against a tree trunk, rubbing his two big toes together, as he often does. A pair of youngsters swing on vines, flashing in and out of an angled shaft of sun. One uses a foot to push off from a tree trunk, spinning himself around. The other swings from vine to vine, Tarzan-style. They are almost painfully cute.

A chimp called Mike lies on his back in a hammock of branches, legs bent, one ankle crossed atop the opposite knee. One arm is behind his head, the other is crooked at the elbow, the hand hanging slack from the wrist, in the manner of a cowboy slouched against a fence. We stare at each other for a full ten seconds. Partly because his pose is so familiarly human and partly because of the way he holds my gaze, I find myself feeling a connection with Mike.

I confess this to Pruetz, who admits to similar feelings. She cares about the Fongoli chimps as one cares about family. She sends excited emails when a baby is born and worries when the elderly and nearly blind Ross disappears for more than a week. But she does not reveal this side of herself at conferences. There it's all lingo and statistics, pairwise affinity indexes and "blended whimper pouts." "Especially with male chimp researchers," she says.

One of the first things primatology students are taught is to avoid anthropomorphism. Because chimps look and act so much like us, it is easy to misread their actions and expressions, to project humanness where it may not belong. For example, I catch Siberut looking toward the sky in what I take to be a contemplative manner, as though pondering life's higher meaning. What he's actually pondering is life's higher saba fruits. Pruetz points some out in the branches above Siberut.

I've been keeping a list of things I have seen or read or heard Pruetz say that drive home this point in unexpected ways. I had not known that chimpanzee yawns are contagious—both among each other and to humans. I had known that chimps laugh, but I did not know that they get upset if someone laughs at them. I knew that captive chimps spit, but I hadn't known that they, like us, seem to consider spitting the most extreme expression of disgust—one reserved, interestingly, for humans. I knew that a captive ape might care for a kitten if you gave one to it, but had not heard of a wild chimpanzee taking one in, as Tia did with a genet kitten. The list goes on. Chimps get up to get snacks in the middle of the night. They lie on their backs and do "the airplane" with their children. They kiss. Shake hands. Pick their scabs before they're ready.

The taboo on anthropomorphizing seems odd, given that the closeness—evolutionary, genetic, and behavioral—between chimpanzees and humans is the very reason we study chimps so obsessively. Some thousand-plus studies have been published on chimpanzees. As a colleague of Pruetz's once said to her, "A chimp takes a crap in the forest, and someone publishes a paper about it." (No exaggeration. One paper has a section on chimpanzees' use of "leaf napkins": "This hygienic technology is directed to their bodily fluids (blood, semen, feces, urine, snot).... Their use ranges from delicate dabbing to vigorous wiping."

Almost blind, deaf, and toothless, Ross is probably in his 40s and too old to hunt. He survives by pounding open fruits—proof that innovation isn't just for the young.

© 1900 JOE MCNALLY/National Geographic Image Collection

As for the chimps, they are not nearly as intrigued by the ape-human connection. While we've been observing them, they have largely ignored us, occasionally shooting a glance over one shoulder as they move through the brush. There is no fear in this glance, but neither is there curiosity or any sort of social overture. It is a glance that says simply, Them again.

Even Mike. He just turned away from my gaze and pointedly, or so it seemed, rolled over to turn his back on me. In hindsight I would have to say that the reason Mike had been looking at me was that I happened to be in his line of vision.

The chimps begin making their nests, breaking off leafy branches and dragging them into the treetops. Pruetz will wait until all are bedded down before turning to head back. We sit and listen to their "nest grunts"—soft, breathy calls that seem to express nothing more than the deep contentment one feels at the end of a day, in a comfortable bed.

Discussion Questions

- What environmental conditions in the savannas of Senegal make the Fongoli chimps particularly valuable in studying the origins of our species? What primate adaptions (i.e. locomotion, food procurement methods, social-structures, etc.) arise from these conditions?
- Pruetz suggests that competition over limited resources "pushed" certain members of the chimp community to "get creative." How might you apply the theory of "ecological intelligence" to the case of the Fongoli chimps and to what aspects of human evolution does this contribute?
- Along the lines of gender and aggression, what traditional views on hunting among the chimpanzees are challenged by the Fongoli chimps? How might this complicate our understanding of our human ancestors?
- Pruetz's research was met with a good deal of resistance. How was her research opposed by other primatologists? Do you think they were justified?

Join the Debate

- Consider the ever-shifting boundaries between chimps and humans as presented by this article. Why is anthropomorphism cautioned against? Conversely, how might it be justified?
- Did the issues raised in this article alter your take on what it means to be human? Following the assertion of Jared Diamond, are humans a type of chimp? Should chimpanzees have animal rights or human rights?

Field Journal: Exploring the Expensive-Tissue Hypothesis

This article makes reference to the Expensive-Tissue Hypothesis by Leslie Aiello and Peter Wheeler, which argues that as encephalization (an increase in brain size) occurs in human and primate species, a corresponding reduction in gut size compensates for the "more expensive" metabolic requirements of larger brains.[1]

Visit your local Natural History museum* with this print-out (http://www.amnh.org/education/resources/rfl/pdf/compare_skeletons.pdf) in your personal field journal.

- Locate the skeletal models for pre-human ancestors (i.e. *A.* afarensis, *H.* erectus, etc.).
- For each skeletal model, observe the brain/gut ratio by recording the relative size and shape of the braincase part of the cranium to the size and shape of the thoracic cavity.

Tip: You may sketch the front and profile views of the brain case and rib cage.

- Compare your observations of the brain/gut ratio between species through evolutionary time.
    - Are your observations consistent with that of Aiello and Wheeler?
    - What other skeletal elements are increased or reduced in size with the enlargement of the brain?
    - What types of behaviors can be linked with these anatomical changes?

---

[1] *Aiello, Leslie C., and Peter Wheeler. 1995. "The Expensive-Tissue Hypothesis: The Brain and the Digestive System in Human and Primate Evolution."* Current Anthropology *36(2): 199–221.*

**Alternatively, you may explore skeletal models by visiting www.eSkeletons.org and www.eFossils.org.*

LAST OF THE NEANDERTHALS

Last of the Neanderthals dispels the decades-old myth of the "simple brutes" and launches them into behavioral modernity independent of anatomically modern human influence. New genetic findings reveal that Neanderthals possessed the ability for language as carriers of the FOXP2 gene and some exhibited red hair and fair skin as expressed by gene MC1R. Current research has yet to discover genetic links or interbreeding of the Neanderthals with Modern Humans and some conjectures are made as to the mysterious disappearance of the species.

As you read "Last of the Neanderthals," consider the following questions:

- In what ways have our understanding of Neanderthals progressed? What remains in question?
- How do genetics and the study of dentition contribute to our knowledge of Neanderthals?
- What lab technologies are used in this article and what type of data do they produce?
- What potential complications and obstacles are involved with the DNA sampling of Neanderthals?
- What arguments are presented in the explanation of the disappearance of the Neanderthals?

For the first time, a Neanderthal female peers from the past in a reconstruction informed by both fossil anatomy and ancient DNA. At least some of her kind carried a gene for red hair and pale skin.

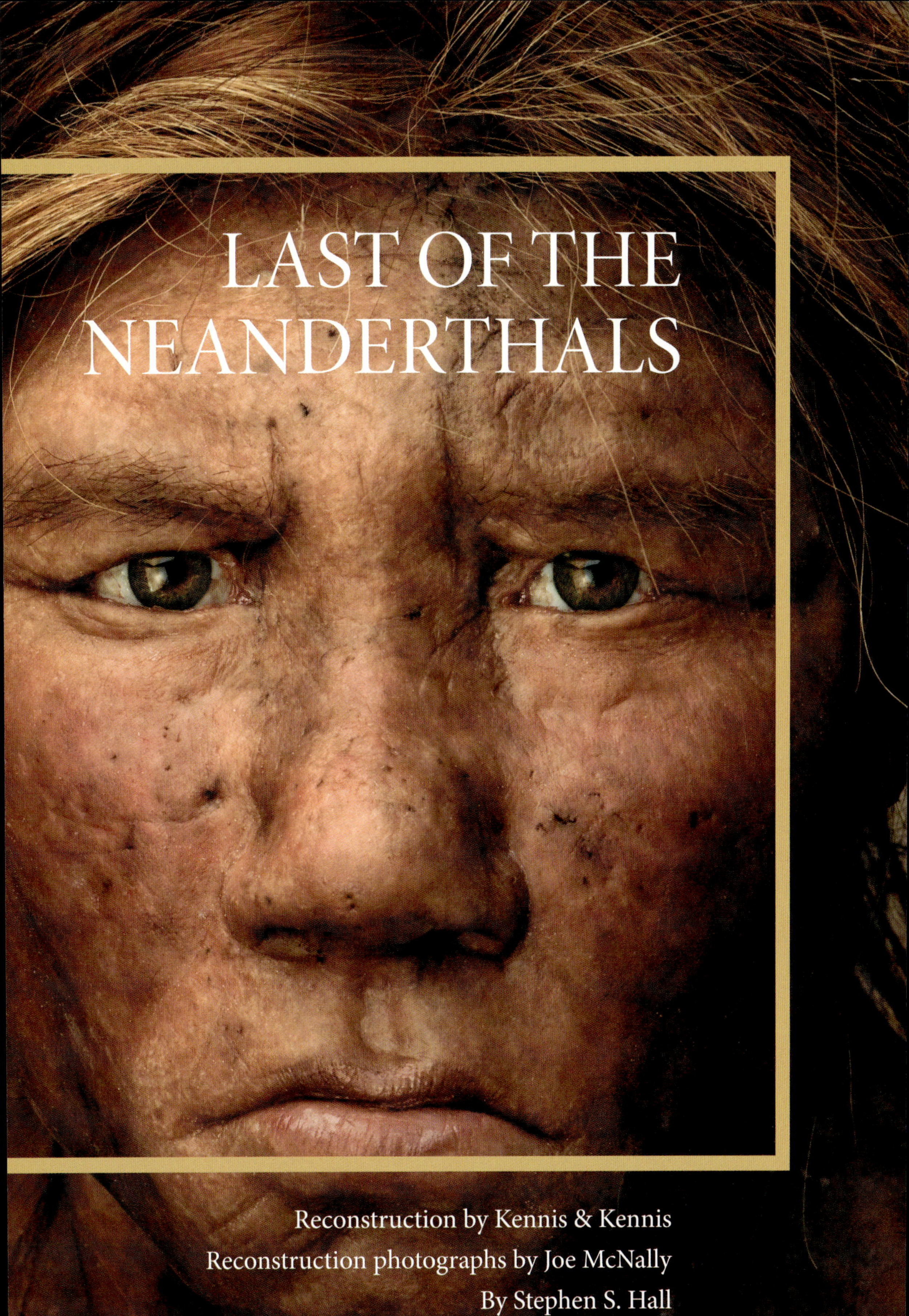

LAST OF THE NEANDERTHALS

Reconstruction by Kennis & Kennis

Reconstruction photographs by Joe McNally

By Stephen S. Hall

A HUNTER RETREATS

With their large brains and enormous strength, Neanderthals seemed equipped to face any obstacle. But as the climate changed and a new kind of human appeared on the landscape, their dwindling numbers sought refuge in the highlands. The heights of northern Spain suggest the demanding environment that confronted many Neanderthals late in their reign. The model grips a spear to signify that females may have hunted with males.

EURASIA WAS THEIRS ALONE FOR 200,000 YEARS. THEN THE NEWCOMERS ARRIVED.

Within another 15,000 years or so, the Neanderthals were gone forever, leaving behind a few bones and a lot of questions.

In March of 1994 some spelunkers exploring an extensive cave system in northern Spain poked their lights into a small side gallery and noticed two human mandibles jutting out of the sandy soil. The cave, called El Sidrón, lay in the midst of a remote upland forest of chestnut and oak trees in the province of Asturias, just south of the Bay of Biscay. Suspecting that the jawbones might date back as far as the Spanish Civil War, when Republican partisans used El Sidrón to hide from Franco's soldiers, the cavers immediately notified the local Guardia Civil. But when police investigators inspected the gallery, they discovered the remains of a much larger—and, it would turn out, much older—tragedy.

Within days, law enforcement officials had shoveled out some 140 bones, and a local judge ordered the remains sent to the national forensic pathology institute in Madrid. By the time scientists finished their analysis (it took the better part of six years), Spain had its earliest cold case. The bones from El Sidrón were not Republican soldiers, but the fossilized remains of a group of Neanderthals who lived, and perhaps died violently, approximately 43,000 years ago. The locale places them at one of the most important geographical intersections of prehistory, and the date puts them squarely at the center of one of the most enduring mysteries in all of human evolution.

The Neanderthals, our closest prehistoric relatives, dominated Eurasia for the better part of 200,000 years. During that time, they poked their famously large and protruding noses into every corner of Europe, and beyond—south along the Mediterranean from the Strait of Gibraltar to Greece and Iraq, north to Russia, as far west as Britain, and almost to Mongolia in the east. Scientists estimate that even at the height of the Neanderthal occupation of western Europe, their total number probably never exceeded 15,000. Yet they managed to endure,

---

Adapted from "Last of the Neanderthals" by Stephen S. Hall: National Geographic Magazine, October 2008.

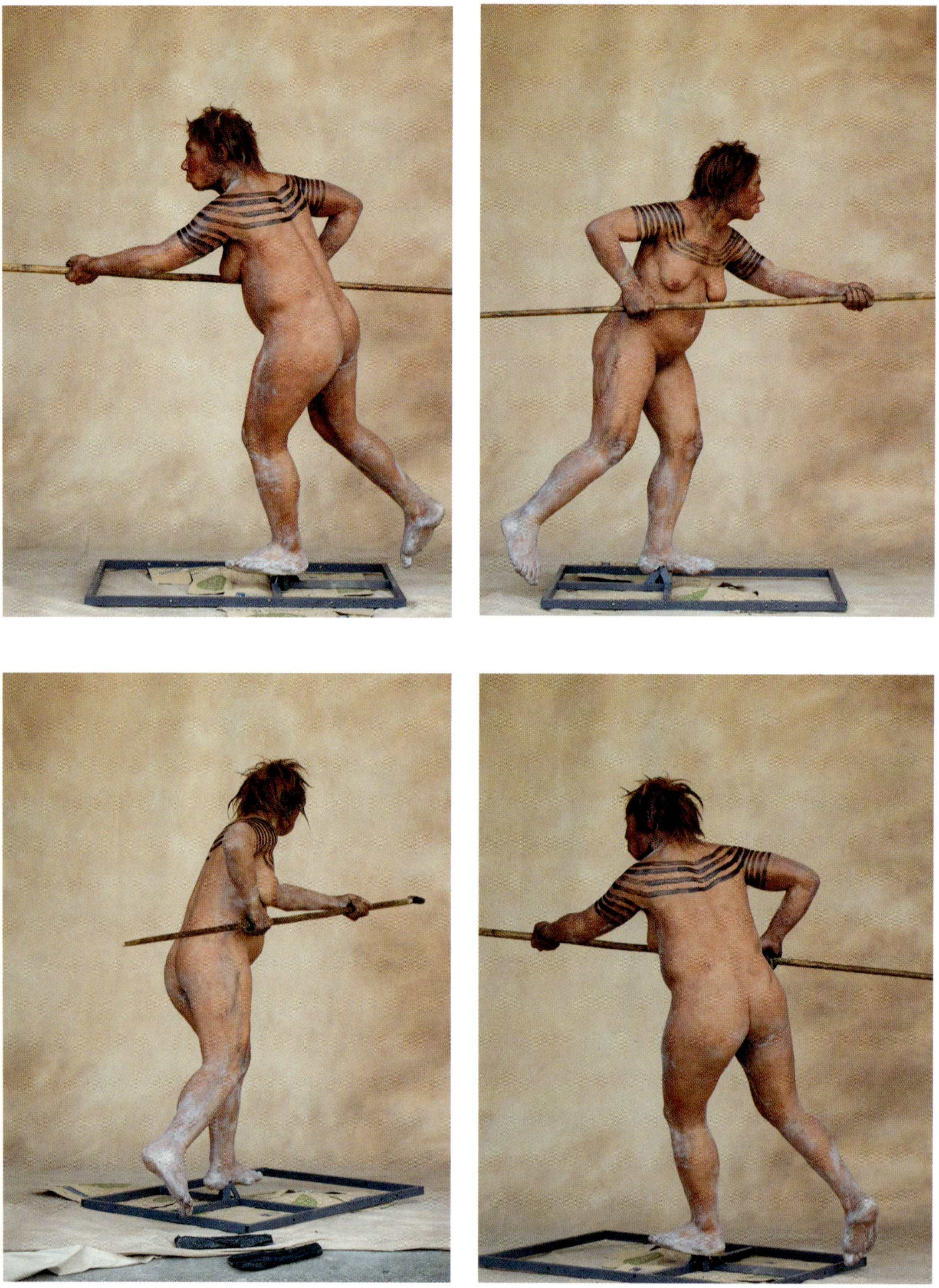

CREATING A NEANDERTHAL

To reconstruct a five-foot-tall, heavily muscled woman, artists Adrie and Alfons Kennis built a skeleton using replicas of a pelvis and cranial anatomy from Neanderthal females combined with parts from a composite skeleton of a male from the American Museum of Natural History in New York. Paleoanthropologist Steve Churchill of Duke University made calculations to reduce male bone sizes to female dimensions. Since summers would have been warm even during glacial periods, Neanderthals probably would have gone naked to shed heat from their stocky bodies. Lumps of pigments found at Neanderthal sites inspired the artists to add decorative body art.

even when a cooling climate turned much of their territory into something like northern Scandinavia today—a frigid, barren tundra, its bleak horizon broken by a few scraggly trees and just enough lichen to keep the reindeer happy.

By the time of the tragedy at El Sidrón, however, the Neanderthals were on the run, seemingly pinned down in Iberia, pockets of central Europe, and along the southern Mediterranean by a deteriorating climate, and further squeezed by the westward spread of anatomically modern humans as they emerged from Africa into the Middle East and beyond. Within another 15,000 years or so, the Neanderthals were gone forever, leaving behind a few bones and a lot of questions. Were they a clever and perseverant breed of survivors, much like us, or a cognitively challenged dead end? What happened during that period, roughly 45,000 to 30,000 years ago, when the Neanderthals shared some parts of the Eurasian landscape with those modern human migrants from Africa? Why did one kind of human being survive, and the other disappear?

On a damp, fog-shrouded morning in September 2007, I stood before the entrance to El Sidrón with Antonio Rosas of the National Museum of Natural Sciences in Madrid, who heads the paleoanthropological investigation. One of his colleagues handed me a flashlight, and I gingerly lowered myself into the black hole. As my eyes adjusted to the interior, I began to make out the fantastic contours of a karstic cave. An underground river had hollowed out a deep vein of sandstone, leaving behind a limestone cavern extending hundreds of yards, with side galleries spidering out to at least 12 entrances. Ten minutes into the cave, I arrived at the Galería del Osario—the "tunnel of bones." Since 2000, some 1,500 bone fragments have been unearthed from this side gallery, representing the remains of at least nine Neanderthals—five young adults, two adolescents, a child of about eight, and a three-year-old toddler. All showed signs of nutritional stress in their teeth—not unusual in young Neanderthals late in their time on Earth. But a deeper desperation is etched in their bones. Rosas picked up a recently unearthed fragment of a skull and another of a long bone of an arm, both with jagged edges.

"These fractures were—clop—made by humans," Rosas said, imitating the blow of a stone tool. "It means these fellows went after the brains and into long bones for the marrow."

In addition to the fractures, cut marks left on the bones by stone tools clearly indicate that the individuals were cannibalized. Whoever ate their flesh, and for whatever reason—starvation? ritual?—the subsequent fate of their remains bestowed upon them a distinct and marvelous kind of immortality. Shortly after the nine individuals died—possibly within days—the ground below them suddenly collapsed, leaving little time for hyenas and other scavengers to scatter the remains. A slurry of bones, sediment, and rocks tumbled 60 feet into a hollow limestone chamber below, much as mud fills the inside walls of a house during a flood.

There, buffered by sand and clay, preserved by the cave's constant temperature, and sequestered in their jewel cases of mineralized bone, a few precious molecules of the Neanderthals' genetic code survived, awaiting a time in the distant future when they could be plucked out, pieced together, and examined for clues to how these people lived, and why they vanished.

The first clue that our kind of human was not the first to inhabit Europe turned up a century and a half ago, about eight miles east of Düsseldorf, Germany. In August 1856 laborers quarrying limestone from a cave in the Neander Valley dug out a beetle-browed skullcap and some thick limb bones. Right from the start, the Neanderthals were saddled with an enduring cultural stereotype as dim-witted, brutish cavemen. The size and shape of the fossils does suggest a short, stout fireplug of a physique *(Continued on page 52)*

PRECIOUS FOSSIL
Suited up to avoid contaminating her find, researcher Araceli Soto Flórez bags a Neanderthal bone from El Sidrón cave in Spain. Fossils uncovered here have yielded faint traces of ancient DNA. Genetic analysis provides evidence for red hair, and perhaps a capacity for speech.

(Continued from page 49) (males averaged about five feet, five inches tall and about 185 pounds), with massive muscles and a flaring rib cage presumably encasing capacious lungs. Steven E. Churchill, a paleoanthropologist at Duke University, has calculated that to support his body mass in a cold climate, a typical Neanderthal male would have needed up to 5,000 calories daily, or approaching what a bicyclist burns each day in the Tour de France. Yet behind its bulging browridges, a Neanderthal's low-domed skull housed a brain with a volume slightly larger on average than our own today. And while their tools and weapons were more primitive than those of the modern humans who supplanted them in Europe, they were no less sophisticated than the implements made by their modern human contemporaries living in Africa and the Middle East.

Were they a clever and perseverant breed of survivors, much like us, or a cognitively challenged dead end?

One of the longest and most heated controversies in human evolution rages around the genetic relationship between Neanderthals and their European successors. Did the modern humans sweeping out of Africa beginning some 60,000 years ago completely replace the Neanderthals, or did they interbreed with them? In 1997 the latter hypothesis was dealt a powerful blow by geneticist Svante Pääbo—then at the University of Munich—who used an arm bone from the original Neanderthal man to deliver it. Pääbo and his colleagues were able to extract a tiny 378-letter snippet of mitochondrial DNA (a kind of short genetic appendix to the main text in each cell) from the 40,000-year-old specimen. When they read out the letters of the code, they found that the specimen's DNA differed from living humans to a degree suggesting that the Neanderthal and modern human lineages had begun to diverge long before the modern human migration out of Africa. Thus the two represent separate geographic and evolutionary branches splitting from a common ancestor. "North of the Mediterranean, this lineage became Neanderthals," said Chris Stringer, research leader on human origins at the Natural History Museum in London, "and south of the Mediterranean, it became us." If there was any interbreeding when they encountered each other later, it was too rare to leave a trace of Neanderthal mitochondrial DNA in the cells of living people.

Pääbo's genetic bombshell seemed to confirm that Neanderthals were a separate species—but it does nothing to solve the mystery of why they vanished, and our species survived.

One obvious possibility is that modern humans were simply more clever, more sophisticated, more "human." Until recently, archaeologists pointed to a "great leap forward" around 40,000 years ago in Europe, when the Neanderthals' relatively humdrum stone tool industry—called Mousterian, after the site of Le Moustier in southwestern France—gave way to the more varied stone and bone tool kits, body ornaments, and other signs of symbolic expression associated with the appearance of modern humans. Some scientists, such as Stanford University anthropologist Richard Klein, still argue for some dramatic genetic change in the brain—possibly associated with a development in language—that propelled early modern humans to cultural dominance at the expense of their beetle-browed forebears.

But the evidence in the ground is not so cut and dried. In 1979 archaeologists discovered a late Neanderthal skeleton at Saint-Césaire in southwestern France surrounded not with typical Mousterian implements, but with a surprisingly modern repertoire of tools. In 1996 Jean-Jacques Hublin of the Max Planck Institute in Leipzig and Fred Spoor of University College London identified a Neanderthal bone in another French cave, near Arcy-sur-Cure, in a layer of sediment also containing ornamental objects previously associated only with modern humans, such as pierced animal teeth and ivory rings. Some scientists, such as British paleoanthropologist Paul Mellars, dismiss such modern "accessorizing" of a fundamentally archaic lifestyle as an "improbable coincidence"—a last gasp of imitative behavior by Neanderthals before the inventive newcomers out of Africa replaced them. But more recently, Francesco d'Errico of the University of Bordeaux and Marie Soressi, also at the Max Planck Institute in Leipzig, analyzed hundreds of crayon-like blocks of manganese dioxide from a French cave called Pech de l'Azé, where Neanderthals lived well before modern humans arrived in Europe. D'Errico and Soressi argue that the Neanderthals used the black pigment for body decoration, demonstrating that they were fully capable of achieving "behavioral modernity" all on their own.

"At the time of the biological transition," says Erik Trinkaus, a paleoanthropologist at Washington University in St. Louis, "the basic behavior [of the two groups] is pretty much the same, and any differences are likely to have been subtle." Trinkaus believes they indeed may have mated occasionally. He sees evidence of admixture between Neanderthals and modern humans in certain fossils, such as a 24,500-year-old skeleton of a young child discovered at the Portuguese site of Lagar Velho, and a 32,000-year-old skull from a cave called Muierii in Romania. "There were very few people on the landscape, and you need to find a mate and reproduce," says Trinkaus. "Why not? Humans are not known to be choosy. Sex happens."

It may have happened, other researchers say, but not often, and not in a way that left behind any evidence. Katerina Harvati, another researcher at the Max Planck Institute in Leipzig, has used detailed 3-D measurements of Neanderthal and early modern human fossils to predict exactly what hybrids between the two would have looked like. None of the fossils examined so far matches her predictions.

The disagreement between Trinkaus and Harvati is hardly the first time that two respected paleoanthropologists have looked at the same set of bones and come up with mutually contradictory interpretations. Pondering—and debating—the meaning of fossil anatomy will always play a role in understanding Neanderthals. But now there are other ways to bring them back to life.

Two days after my first descent into El Sidrón cave, Araceli Soto Flórez, a graduate student at the University of Oviedo, came across a fresh Neanderthal bone, probably a fragment of a femur. All digging immediately ceased, and most of the crew evacuated the chamber. Soto Flórez then squeezed herself into a sterile jumpsuit, gloves, booties, and plastic face mask. Under the watchful eyes of Antonio Rosas and molecular biologist Carles Lalueza-Fox, she delicately extracted the bone from the soil, placed it in a sterile plastic bag, and deposited the bag in a chest of ice. After a brief stop in a hotel freezer in nearby Villamayo, the leg bone eventually arrived at Lalueza-Fox's laboratory at the Institute of Evolutionary Biology in Barcelona. His interest was not in the anatomy of the leg or anything it might reveal about Neanderthal locomotion. All he wanted from it was its DNA.

Prehistoric cannibalism has been very good for modern-day molecular biology. Scraping flesh from a bone also removes the DNA of microorganisms that might otherwise contaminate the sample. The bones of El Sidrón have not yielded the most DNA of any Neanderthal fossil—that honor belongs to a specimen from Croatia, also cannibalized—but so far they have revealed the most compelling insights into Neanderthal appearance and behavior. In October 2007 Lalueza-Fox, Holger Römpler of the University of Leipzig, and their colleagues announced that they had isolated a pigmentation gene from the DNA of an individual at El Sidrón (as well as another Neanderthal fossil from Italy). The particular form of the gene, called MC1R, indicated that at least some Neanderthals would have had red hair, pale skin, and, possibly, freckles. The gene is unlike that of red-haired people today,

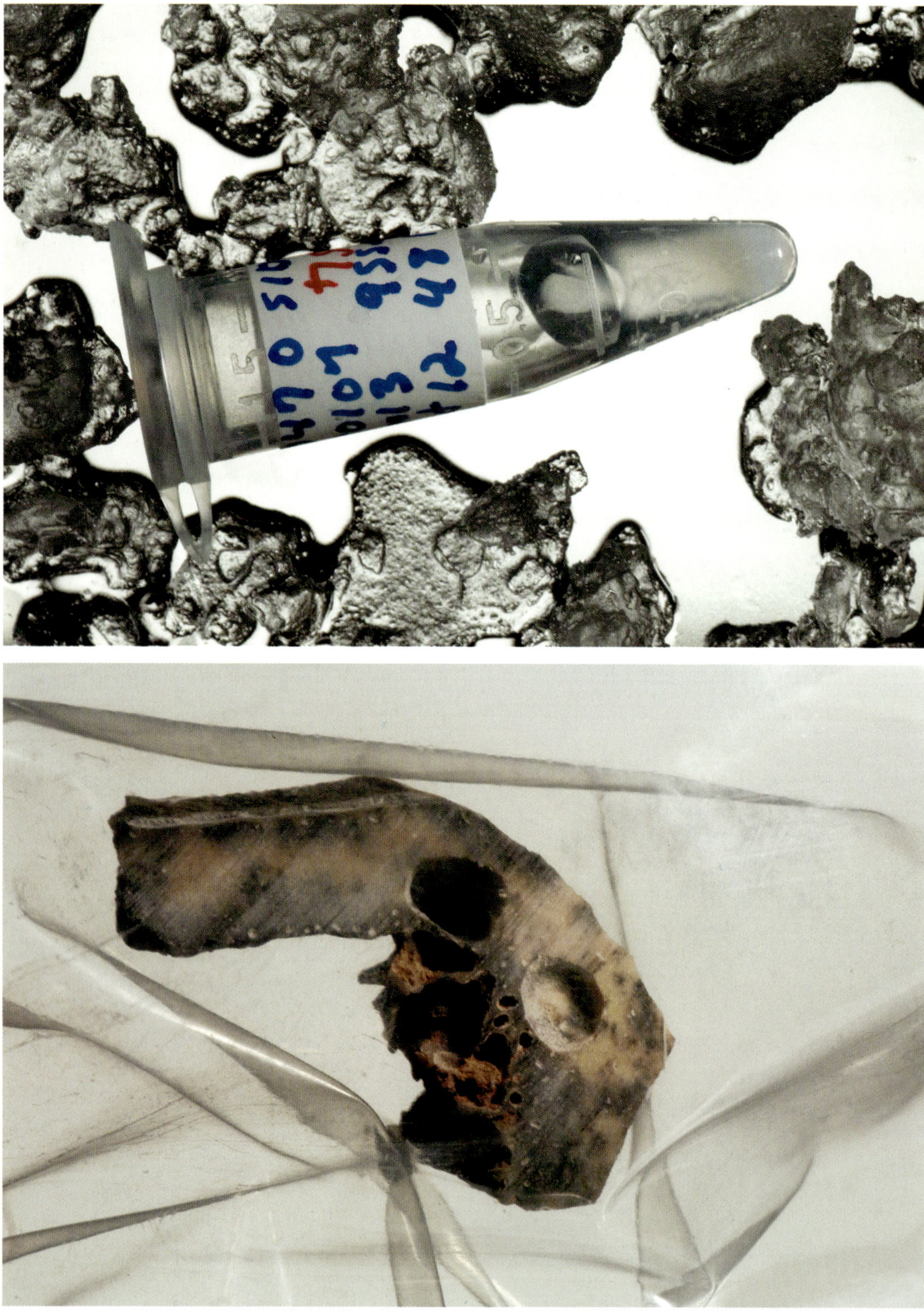

GENETIC ESSENCE

Taking DNA from a 38,000-year-old leg bone fragment (bottom) found in Croatia, scientists are spelling out the complete Neanderthal genetic code. Results from the sample (top, on ice) suggest that Neanderthals and modern humans are separate species, but do not rule out some interbreeding.

however—suggesting that Neanderthals and modern humans developed the trait independently, perhaps under similar pressures in northern latitudes to evolve fair skin to let in more sunlight for the manufacture of vitamin D. Just a few weeks earlier, Svante Pääbo, who now heads the genetics laboratory at the Max Planck Institute in Leipzig, Lalueza-Fox, and their colleagues had announced an even more astonishing find: Two El Sidrón individuals appeared to share, with modern humans, a version of a gene called FOXP2 that contributes to speech and language ability, acting not only in the brain but also on the nerves that control facial muscles. Whether Neanderthals were capable of sophisticated language abilities or a more primitive form of vocal communication (singing, for example) still remains unclear, but the new genetic findings suggest they possessed some of the same vocalizing hardware as modern humans.

Behind its bulging browridges, a Neanderthal's skull housed a brain slightly larger on average than our own today.

All this from a group of ill-fated Neanderthals buried in a cave collapse, soon after they were consumed by their own kind.

"So maybe it's a good thing to eat your conspecifics," says Pääbo.

A tall, cheerful Swede, Pääbo is the main engine behind a breathtaking scientific tour de force: the attempt, expected to be completed next month, to read out not just single Neanderthal genes, but the entire three-billion-letter sequence of the Neanderthal genome. Traces of DNA in fossils are vanishingly faint, and because Neanderthal DNA is ever so close to that of living people, one of the biggest hurdles in sequencing it is the ever present threat of contamination by modern human DNA—especially by the scientists handling the specimens. The precautions taken in excavating at El Sidrón are now becoming standard practice at other Neanderthal sites. Most of the DNA for Pääbo's genome project, however, has come from the Croatian specimen, a 38,000-year-old fragment of leg bone found almost 30 years ago in the Vindija cave. Originally deemed unimportant, it sat in a drawer in Zagreb, largely untouched and thus uncontaminated, for most of its museum life.

Now it is the equivalent of a gold mine for prehistoric human DNA, albeit an extremely difficult mine to work. After the DNA is extracted in a sterile laboratory in the basement of the Max Planck Institute, it is shipped overnight to Branford, Connecticut, where collaborators at 454 Life Sciences have invented machines that can rapidly decipher the sequence of DNA's chemical letters. The vast majority of those letters spell out bacterial contaminants or other non-Neanderthal genetic information. But in the fall of 2006, Pääbo and his colleagues announced they had deciphered approximately one million letters of Neanderthal DNA. (At the same time, a second group, headed by Edward Rubin at the Department of Energy Joint Genome Institute in Walnut Creek, California, used DNA provided by Pääbo to read out snippets of genetic code using a different approach.) By last year, dogged by claims that their work had serious contamination problems, the Leipzig group claimed to have improved accuracy and identified about 70 million letters of DNA—roughly 2 percent of the total.

"We know that the human and chimpanzee sequences are 98.7 percent the same, and Neanderthals are much closer to us than chimps," said Ed Green, head of biomathematics in Pääbo's group in Leipzig, "so the reality is that for most of the sequence, there's no difference between Neanderthals and [modern] humans." But the differences—less than a half percent of the sequence—are enough to confirm that the two lineages had begun to diverge around 700,000 years ago. The Leipzig group also managed to extract mitochondrial DNA from two fossils of uncertain origin that had been excavated in Uzbekistan and southern Siberia; both had a uniquely Neanderthal genetic signature. While the Uzbekistan specimen, a young boy, had long been considered a Neanderthal, the Siberian specimen was a huge surprise, extending the known Neanderthal range some 1,200 miles east of their European stronghold.

So, while the new genetic evidence appears to confirm that Neanderthals were a separate species from us, it also suggests that they may have possessed human language and were successful over a far larger sweep of Eurasia than previously thought. Which brings us back to the same hauntingly persistent question that has shadowed them from the beginning: Why did they disappear?

To coax a Neanderthal fossil to reveal its secrets, you can measure it with calipers, probe it with a CT scan, or try to capture the ghost of its genetic code. Or if you happen to have at your disposal a type of particle accelerator called a synchrotron, you can put it in a lead-lined room and blast it with a 50,000-volt x-ray beam, without disturbing so much as a single molecule.

Over a sleep-deprived week in October 2007, a team of scientists gathered at the European Synchrotron Radiation Facility (ESRF) in Grenoble, France, for an unprecedented "convention of jawbones." The goal was to explore a crucial question in the life history of the Neanderthals: Did they reach maturity at an earlier age than their modern human counterparts? If so, it might have implications for their brain development, which in turn might help explain why they disappeared. The place to look for answers was deep inside the structure of Neanderthal teeth.

"When I was young, I thought that teeth were not so useful in assessing recent human evolution, but now I think they are the most important thing," said Jean-Jacques Hublin, who had accompanied his Max Planck Institute colleague Tanya Smith to Grenoble.

Along with Paul Tafforeau of the ESRF, Hublin and Smith were squeezed into a computer-filled hutch at the facility—one of the three largest synchrotrons in the world, with a storage ring for energized electrons half a mile in circumference—watching on a video monitor as the x-ray beam zipped through the right upper canine of an adolescent Neanderthal from the site of Le Moustier in southwestern France, creating arguably the most detailed dental x-ray in human history. Meanwhile, a dream team of other fossils sat on a shelf nearby, awaiting their turn in the synchrotron's spotlight: two jawbones of Neanderthal juveniles recovered in Krapina, Croatia, dating back 130,000 to 120,000 years; the so-called La Quina skull from a Neanderthal youth, discovered in France and dating from between 75,000 to 40,000 years ago; and two striking 90,000-year-old modern human specimens, teeth intact, found in a rock shelter called Qafzeh in Israel.

When teeth are imaged at high resolution, they reveal a complex, three-dimensional hatch of daily and longer periodic growth lines, like tree rings, along with stress lines that encode key moments in an individual's life history. The trauma of birth etches a sharp neonatal stress line on the enamel; the time of weaning and episodes of nutritional deprivation or other environmental stresses similarly leave distinct marks on developing teeth. "Teeth preserve a continuous, permanent record of growth, from before birth until they finish growing at the end of adolescence," Smith explained. Human beings take longer to reach puberty than chimpanzees, our nearest living relatives—which means more time spent learning and developing within the context of the social group. Early hominin species that lived on the savanna in Africa millions of years ago matured fast, more like chimps. So when in evolution did the longer modern pattern begin?

To address this question, Smith, Tafforeau, and colleagues had previously used the synchrotron to demonstrate that an early modern human child from a site called Jebel Irhoud in Morocco (dated to around 160,000 years ago) showed the modern human life history pattern. In contrast, the "growth rings" in the 100,000-year-old tooth of a young Neanderthal discovered in *(Continued on page 61)*

Side by Side With Neanderthals

hen our ancestors emerged from Africa into Eurasia around 45,000 years ago, they found the landscape ready inhabited. Neanderthals were 99.5 percent genetically identical to modern humans, but had evolved stinctive anatomy during hundreds of thousands of years in the cold Eurasian climate.

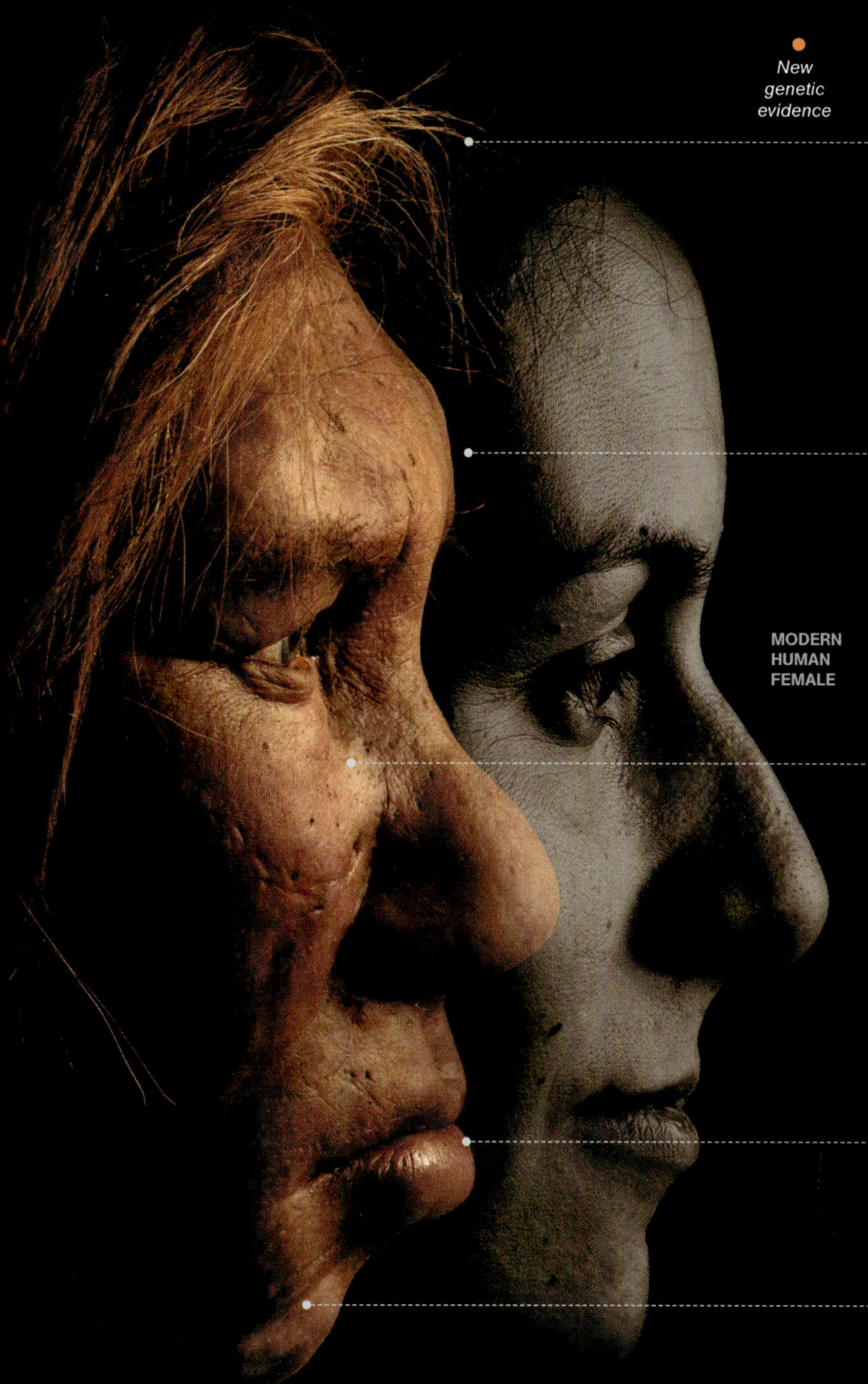

Robust Bodies Adapted to the Cc

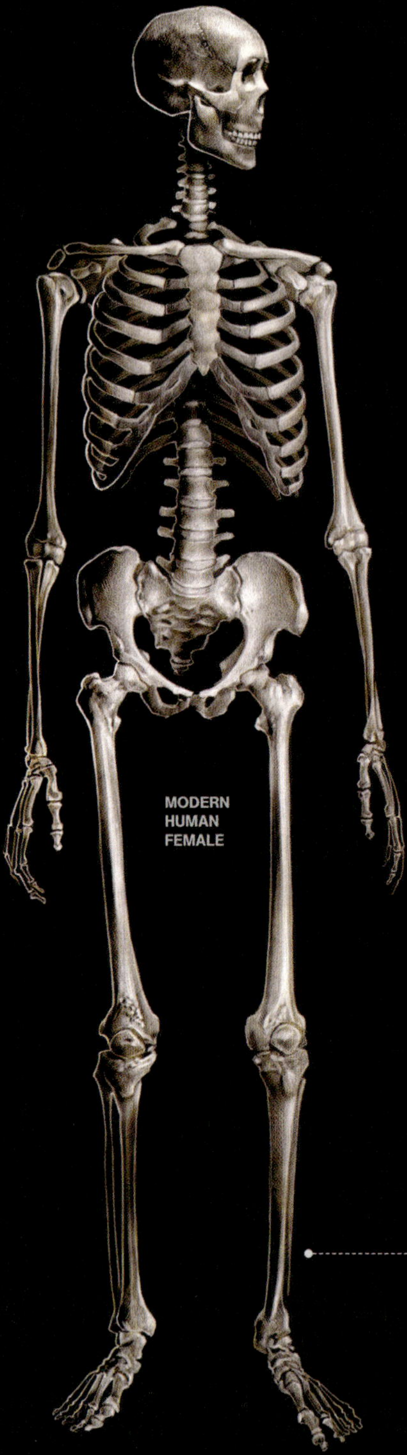

NEANDERTHAL SKELETON

Neanderthal skulls were long and low, but held brains slightly larger on average than those of living humans.

Wide bodies conserved heat in cold climates, while large, conical rib cages housed big lungs needed for high levels of activity.

Sturdy, heavily muscled limb bones evolved in response to a demanding lifestyle.

Large muscles positioned to maximize leverage resulted in exceptional strength.

Short limbs helped reduce surface area to retain body heat.

DAILY CALORIC NEEDS

2,200 cal/day

** USDA recommendation for female of average size (5'4" tall, 138 pounds) who engages in light-to-moderate activity*

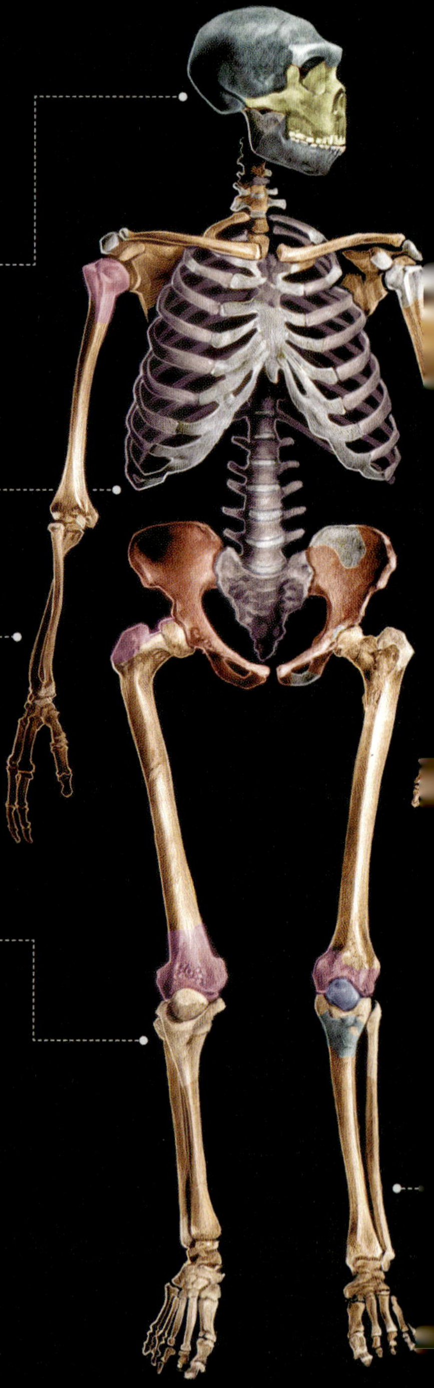

RECONSTRUCTION

The female Neanderthal illustrated in this story was created by assembling casts of fossil bones from several individuals, including rescaled male specimens.

- SPY 1 (BELGIUM)
- GIBRALTAR (U.K.)
- LA FERRASSIE 1 (FRANCE)
- KEBARA 2 (ISRAEL)
- TABUN 1 (ISRAEL) THE PELVIS PORTION ON THE LEFT WAS CREATED BY MIRRORING THE EXISTING FOSSIL ON THE RIGHT
- FELDHOFER 1 (NEANDER VALLEY, GERMANY)
- LA CHAPELLE-AUX-SAINTS (FRANCE)
- RECONSTRUCTED FROM MODERN HUMANS

4,034 cal/day

nderthal
ale of average
(5'2" tall,
pounds)

Diverging Lineages

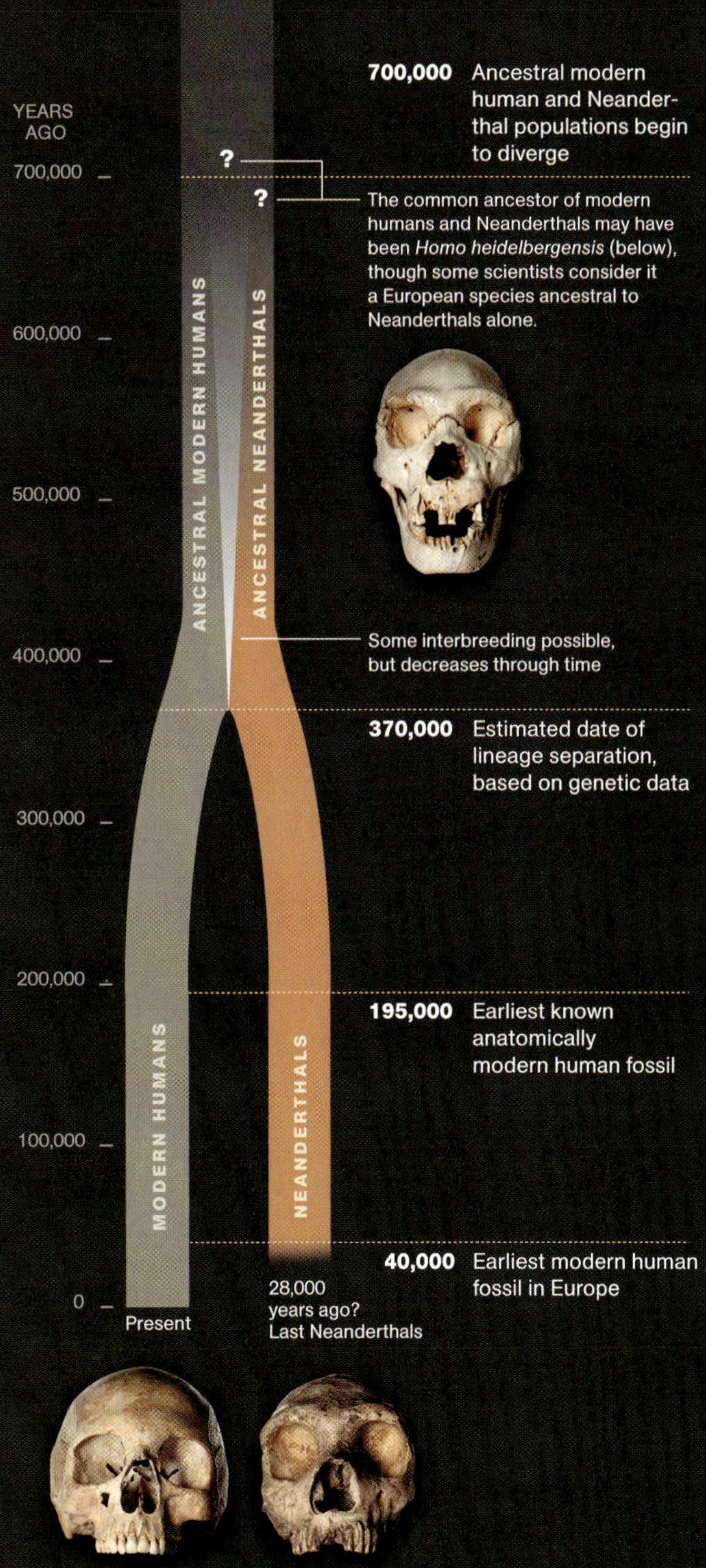

JUAN VELASCO, NG STAFF. ART BY BRUCE MORSER. SOURCES: STEVEN E. CHURCHILL, DUKE UNIVERSITY; CHRIS STRINGER, NATURAL HISTORY MUSEUM, LONDON; ERIK TRINKAUS, WASHINGTON UNIVERSITY IN ST. LOUIS; BONE CLONES, INC. SKULLS PHOTOGRAPHED AT: BURGOS MUSEUM (TOP); NATURAL HISTORY MUSEUM, LONDON (BOTTOM, BOTH)

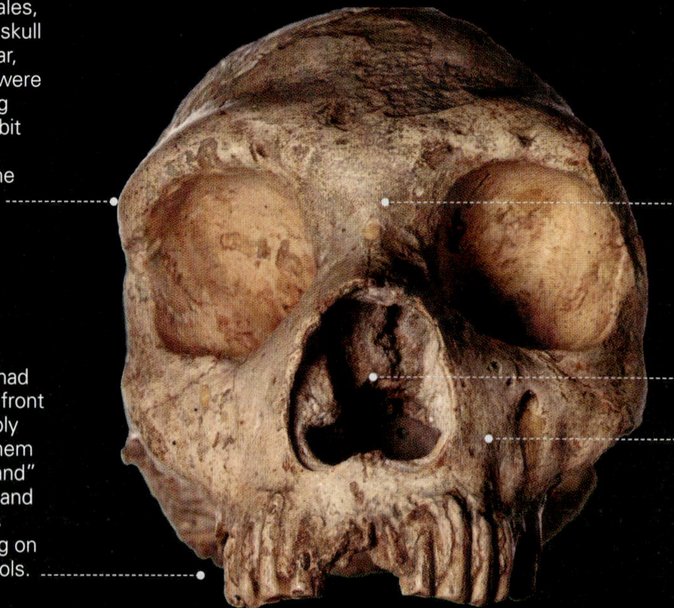

NEANDERTHAL SKULL

MODERN HUMAN SKULL

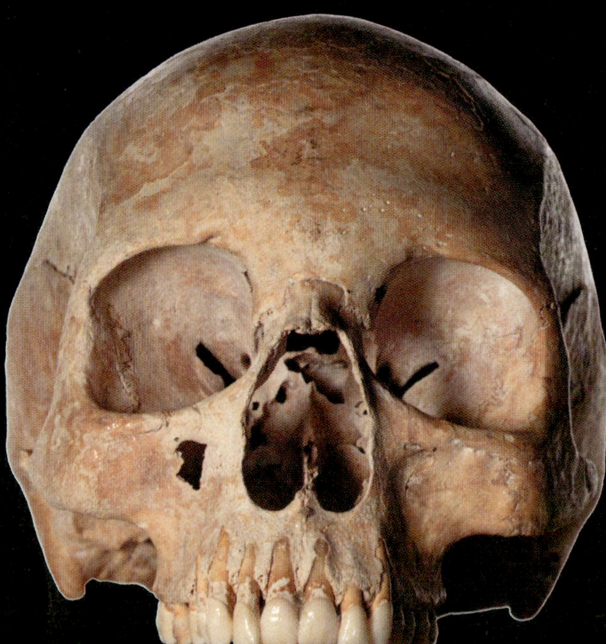

(Continued from page 56) the Scladina cave in Belgium indicated that the child was eight years old when it died and appeared to be on track to reach puberty several years sooner than the average for modern humans. Another research team, using a single Neanderthal tooth, had found no such difference between its growth pattern and that of living humans. But while a full analysis from the "jawbone convention" would take time, preliminary results, Smith said, were "consistent with what we see in Scladina."

> Their bodies' relentless demand for calories probably forced Neanderthal women and children to join in the hunt.

"This would certainly affect Neanderthal social organization, mating strategy, and parenting behavior," says Hublin. "Imagine a society where individuals start to reproduce four years earlier than in modern humans. It's a very different society. It could also mean the Neanderthals' cognitive abilities may have been different from modern humans."

Neanderthal society may have differed in another way crucial to group survival: what archaeologists call cultural buffering. A buffer is something in a group's behavior—a technology, a form of social organization, a cultural tradition—that hedges its bets in the high-stakes game of natural selection. It's like having a small cache of extra chips at your elbow in a poker game, so you don't have to fold your hand quite as soon. For example, Mary Stiner and Steven Kuhn of the University of Arizona argue that early modern humans emerged from Africa with the buffer of an economically efficient approach to hunting and gathering that resulted in a more diverse diet. While men chased after large animals, women and children foraged for small game and plant foods. Stiner and Kuhn maintain that Neanderthals did not enjoy the benefits of such a marked division of labor. From southern Israel to northern Germany, the archaeological record shows that Neanderthals instead relied almost entirely on hunting big and medium-size mammals like horses, deer, bison, and wild cattle. No doubt they were eating some vegetable material and even shellfish near the Mediterranean, but the lack of milling stones or other evidence for processing plant foods suggests to Stiner and Kuhn that to a Neanderthal vegetables were supplementary foods, "more like salads, snacks, and desserts than energy-rich staple foods."

Their bodies' relentless demand for calories, especially in higher latitudes and during colder interludes, probably forced Neanderthal women and children to join in the hunt—a "rough and dangerous business," write Stiner and Kuhn, judging by the many healed fractures evident on Neanderthal upper limbs and skulls. The modern human bands that arrived on the landscape toward the end of the Neanderthals' time had other options.

"By diversifying diet and having personnel who [did different tasks], you have a formula for spreading risk, and that is ultimately good news for pregnant women and for kids," Stiner told me. "So if one thing falls through, there's something else." A Neanderthal woman would have been powerful and resilient. But without such cultural buffering, she and her young would have been at a disadvantage.

Of all possible cultural buffers, perhaps the most important was the cushion of society itself. According to Erik Trinkaus, a Neanderthal social unit would have been about the size of an extended family. But in early modern human sites in Europe, Trinkaus said, "we start getting sites that represent larger populations." Simply living in a larger group has biological as well as social repercussions. Larger groups inevitably demand more social interactions, which goads the brain into greater activity during childhood and adolescence, creates pressure to increase the sophistication of language, and indirectly increases the average life span of group members. Longevity, in turn, increases intergenerational transmission of knowledge and (Continued on page 65)

Marina Allende, from a farm near El Sidrón, where Neanderthals once roamed, displays how a modern European woman sizes up next to the shorter, thicker Neanderthal physique. Neanderthals' fur robes were likely crude, as no evidence exists of sewing tools.

RISE AND FALL OF NEANDERTHALS

Recent genetic evidence reveals that Neanderthals occupied a wider swath of territory than previously thought, settling as far east as Siberia (top). Some 45,000 years ago, anatomically modern humans from Africa migrated into Eurasia (bottom). Climate swings and competition with the newcomers may have combined to push Neanderthals into a few outposts before they went extinct.

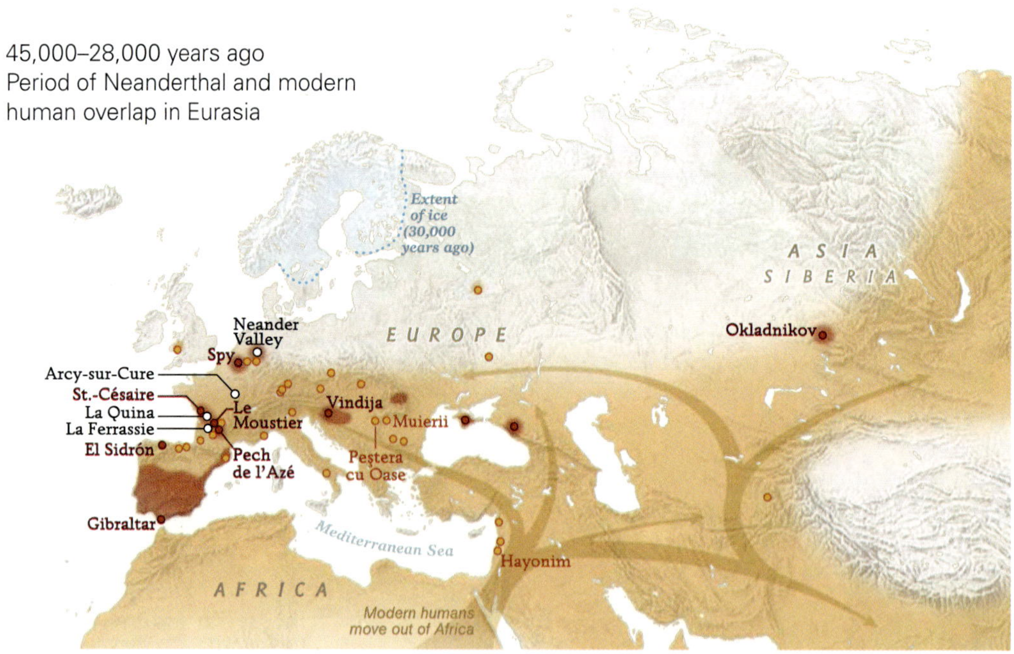

SOURCES: WILLIAM DAVIES, UNIVERSITY OF SOUTHHAMPTON; CLIVE FINLAYSON, GIBRALTAR MUSEUM; CHRIS STRINGER, NATURAL HISTORY MUSEUM, LONDON.

© Charles Berry/Lisa Ritter/National Geographic Image Collection

EVOLVING TOOL KIT
With edges both sharp and durable, a heavy, well-used flint tool (left) probably served its Neanderthal owner as both a hide scraper and the point of a thrusting spear. Neanderthals advanced the art of toolmaking with their method of preparing carefully shaped stone cores, from which they flaked off pieces of size and weight suitable for diverse tools. Lacking projectile weapons, however, they had to engage large prey at close quarters. Modern humans brought lighter, more specialized tools to Europe—including narrow flint blades (right) that could have been hafted to a throwing spear, making hunting more efficient and less dangerous.

© 2008 DAVID LIITTSCHWAGER/National Geographic Image Collection

(Continued from page 61) creates what Chris Stringer calls a "culture of innovation"—the passage of practical survival skills and toolmaking technology from one generation to the next, and later between one group and another.

Whatever the suite of cultural buffers, they may well have provided an extra, albeit thin, layer of insulation against the harsh climatic stresses that Stringer argues peaked right around the time the Neanderthals vanished. Ice core data suggest that from about 30,000 years ago until the last glacial maximum about 18,000 years ago, the Earth's climate fluctuated wildly, sometimes within the space of decades. A few more people in the social unit, with a few more skills, might have given modern humans an edge when conditions turned harsh. "Not a vast edge," Stringer said. "Neanderthals were obviously well adapted to a colder climate. But with the superimposition of these extreme changes in climate on the competition with modern humans, I think that made the difference."

Which leaves the final, delicate—and, as Jean-Jacques Hublin likes to say, politically incorrect—question that has bedeviled Neanderthal studies since the Out of Africa theory became generally accepted: Was the replacement by modern humans attenuated and peaceful, the Pleistocene version of kissing cousins, or was it relatively swift and hostile?

"Most Neanderthals and modern humans probably lived most of their lives without seeing each other," he said, carefully choosing his words. "The way I imagine it is that occasionally in these border areas, some of these guys would see each other at a distance…but I think the most likely thing is that they excluded each other from the landscape. Not just avoided, but excluded. We know from recent research on hunter-gatherers that they are much less peaceful than generally believed."

"Sometimes I just turn out the lights in here and think what it must have been like for them."

Evolutionary biologist Clive Finlayson, of the Gibraltar Museum, was standing in the vestibule of Gorham's Cave, a magnificent tabernacle of limestone opening to the sea on the Rock of Gibraltar. Inside, fantastic excretions of flowstone drooled from the ceiling of the massive nave. The stratigraphy in the cave is pocked with evidence of Neanderthal occupation going back 125,000 years, including stone

EATING THEIR OWN

Cut marks on a Neanderthal jawbone, made when flesh was stripped off with a stone tool, testify to an act of cannibalism. All nine skeletons from El Sidrón show such signs of defleshing. Evidence of cannibalism—to satisfy hunger, or perhaps as a ritual practice—is not uncommon in Neanderthal fossils.

© 2008 DAVID LIITTSCHWAGER/National Geographic Image Collection

spearpoints and scrapers, charred pine nuts, and the remains of ancient hearths. Two years ago, Finlayson and his colleagues used radiocarbon dating to determine that the embers in some of those fireplaces died out only 28,000 years ago—the last known trace of Neanderthals on Earth. (Other hearths in the cave may be as young as 24,000 years old, but their dating is controversial.)

From pollen and animal remains, Finlayson has reconstructed what the environment was like from 50,000 to 30,000 years ago. Back then, a narrow coastal shelf surrounded Gibraltar, the Mediterranean two or three miles distant. The landscape was scrub savanna scented with rosemary and thyme, its rolling sand dunes interrupted by the occasional cork oak and stone pine, with wild asparagus growing in the coastal flats. Prehistoric vultures, some with nine-foot wingspans, nested high up in the cliff face, scanning the dunes for meals. Finlayson imagines the Neanderthals watching the birds circle and descend, then racing them for food. Their diet was certainly more varied than the typical Neanderthal dependence on terrestrial game. His research team has found rabbit bones, tortoise shells, and mussels in the cave, along with dolphin bones and a seal skeleton with cut marks. "Except for rice, you've almost got a Mousterian paella!" Finlayson joked.

But then things changed. When the coldest fingers of the Ice Age finally reached southern Iberia in a series of abrupt fluctuations between 30,000 and 23,000 years ago, the landscape was transformed into a semiarid steppe. On this more open playing field, perhaps the tall, gracile modern humans moving into the region with projectile spears gained the advantage over the stumpy, muscle-bound Neanderthals. But Finlayson argues that it was not so much the arrival of modern humans as the dramatic shifts in climate that pushed the Iberian Neanderthals to the brink. "A three-year period of intense cold, or a landslide, when you're down to ten people, could

DENTAL EXAM

The perfect teeth in a 42,000-year-old jawbone from Le Moustier in France offer an opportunity to probe into the nature of Neanderthal adolescence. Scientists penetrated the upper right canine with x-ray beams generated in a synchrotron particle accelerator in Grenoble, France, revealing daily growth lines between thicker eight-day bands in the tooth's enamel. The evidence pinpoints when the subject died, sometime right before or after his 12th birthday. For a young person, the molars were quite well developed, suggesting shorter childhoods for Neanderthals—and less time for brains to develop in the context of the social group.

© 2008 DAVID LIITTSCHWAGER/National Geographic Image Collection

be enough," he said. "Once you reach a certain level, you're the living dead."

The larger point may be that the demise of the Neanderthals is not a sprawling yet coherent paleoanthropological novel; rather, it is a collection of related, but unique, short stories of extinction. "Why did the Neanderthals disappear in Mongolia?" Stringer asked. "Why did they disappear in Israel? Why did they disappear in Italy, in Gibraltar, in Britain? Well, the answer could be different in different places, because it probably happened at different times. So we're talking about a large range, and a disappearance and retreat at different times, with pockets of Neanderthals no doubt surviving in different places at different

One night some 28,000 years ago in Gibraltar, a small group of Neanderthals built a fire in Gorham's Cave (at center). Their charcoal and stone tools are the last known signs of Neanderthal life.

© 2008 DAVID LIITTSCHWAGER/National Geographic Image Collection

times. Gibraltar is certainly one of their last outposts. It could be the last, but we don't know for sure."

Whatever happened, the denouement of all these stories had a signatory in Gorham's Cave. In a deep recess of the cavern, not far from that last Neanderthal hearth, Finlayson's team recently discovered several red handprints on the wall, a sign that modern humans had arrived in Gibraltar. Preliminary analysis of the pigments dates the handprints between 20,300 and 19,500 years ago. "It's like they were saying, Hey, it's a new world now," said Finlayson.

Discussion Questions

- What physical evidence leads people to believe that Neanderthals were "unintelligent brutes" and what evidence suggests that they were culturally and behaviorally modern in their own right?
- What lines of evidence suggest that Neanderthals were a separate species from our modern human forebears? Did interbreeding occur?
- What evidence supports the hypothesis that Neanderthals had to withstand harsh living conditions?
- What investigative methods and technologies were used in uncovering information about Neanderthals? What types of information can be derived from studying teeth?
- According to the article, what hypotheses explain the extinction of the Neanderthals?

Join the Debate

Concerning the highly debated ancestral ties to the Neanderthals, as discussed in this article, why was the idea met with such resistance? Do you believe that the early resistance to this idea would be different if it was known, then, that Neanderthals can be considered behaviorally modern? What does this imply about the importance we place on "the origins story" and genetic/biological evidence?

Field Journal: Shifting Paradigms of *Homo* neanderthalensis

As the field of Physical Anthropology grows in sophistication—new methods and technologies are developed, biases and ethical considerations are taken into account, and new information is uncovered—it becomes necessary to reevaluate past interpretations of the fossil and archaeological record. As mentioned in this article, Neanderthals are increasingly credited for behavioral modernity and symbolic thought.

- Look up the following Neanderthal sites in your textbooks or on the web: La Chapelle-aux-Saints I (France); Shanidar I and IV (Iraq); La Ferrassie (France); and Amud Cave (Israel).
- Examine the fossil and artifactual evidence and determine what that may reasonably demonstrate about "behavioral modernity" (e.g., care of the injured or elderly, burial offerings, rituals, etc.). What new questions and interpretations can you offer?

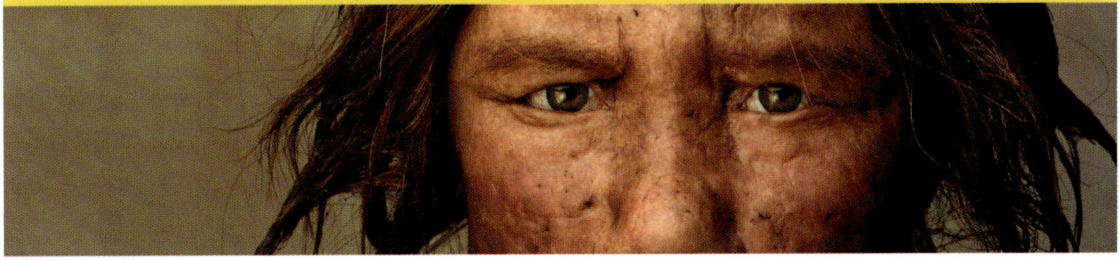

THE PEOPLE TIME FORGOT

The People Time Forgot covers the highly controversial *Homo* floresiensis remains discovered in 2003 at Liang Bua Cave in Flores, Indonesia. This newly proposed species of *Homo* is likened to erectus/ergaster fossils but has "Hobbit-like" proportions. Appearing relatively recent, nearly 11,000 years ago, these small-brained ancestors are associated with the use of fire and sophisticated tools.

As you read "The People Time Forgot," consider the following questions:

- What are the physical attributes of *H.* floresiensis and why is it considered a new species?
- How might they have arrived on the Island of Flores?
- What artifacts were found in association with *H.* floresiensis?
- How are the remains contested?
- What information is based on conjecture and what information is based on material fact?

THE PEOPLE TIME FORGOT

By Mike Morwood • Thomas Sutikna • Richard Roberts

Photographs by Kenneth Garrett • Art by Lars Grant-West

Thomas Sutikna of the Indonesian Centre for Archaeology holds a skull that he and fellow scientists believe represents a new human species, Homo floresiensis. *Found in a cave on Flores, the species existed alongside modern humans as recently as 13,000 years ago, yet may descend from* Homo erectus, *which arose some two million years ago.*

© 2005 Ira Block/National Geographic Image Collection

MINIATURE BEINGS WITH SKULLS FAR SMALLER THAN OUR OWN

SPRANG FROM AN ANCIENT LINE OF HUMAN ANCESTORS.

HOW DID THEY REACH—AND SURVIVE ON—A REMOTE INDONESIAN ISLAND?

> **We had discovered a new kind of human.**

At first we thought it was a child, perhaps three years old. But a closer look showed that the tiny, fragile bones we had just laid bare in a spacious cave on the Indonesian island of Flores belonged to a full-grown adult just over three feet tall.

Had we simply found a modern human stunted by disease or malnutrition? No. The bones looked primitive, and other remains from Liang Bua, which means "cool cave" in the local Manggarai language, showed that this skeleton wasn't unique. It was typical of a whole population of tiny beings who once lived on this remote island. We had discovered a new kind of human.

Back in the lab, where we analyzed the bones and other artifacts, the full dimensions of what we had discovered began to emerge. This tiny human relative, whom we nicknamed Hobbit, lived just 18,000 years ago, a time when modern humans—people like us—were on the march around the globe. Yet it looked more like a diminutive version of human ancestors a hundred times older, from the other end of Asia.

We had stumbled on a lost world: pygmy survivors from an earlier era, hanging on far from the main currents of human prehistory. Who were they? And what does this lost relative tell us about our evolutionary past?

A 220-mile-long island between mainland Asia and Australia, Flores was never connected by land bridges to either continent. Even at times of low sea level, island-hopping to Flores from mainland Asia involved sea crossings of up to 15 miles. Before modern humans began ferrying animals such as monkeys, pigs, and dogs to the island about 4,000 years ago, the only land mammals to reach it were stegodonts (extinct elephant ancestors) and rodents—the former by swimming and the latter by hitching a ride on flotsam. No people could have reached Flores until modern humans came along, with the brainpower needed to build boats. Or so most scientists believed. *(Continued on page 82)*

Adapted from "The People Time Forgot" by Mike Morwood, Thomas Sutikna, and Richard Roberts: National Geographic Magazine, April 2005.

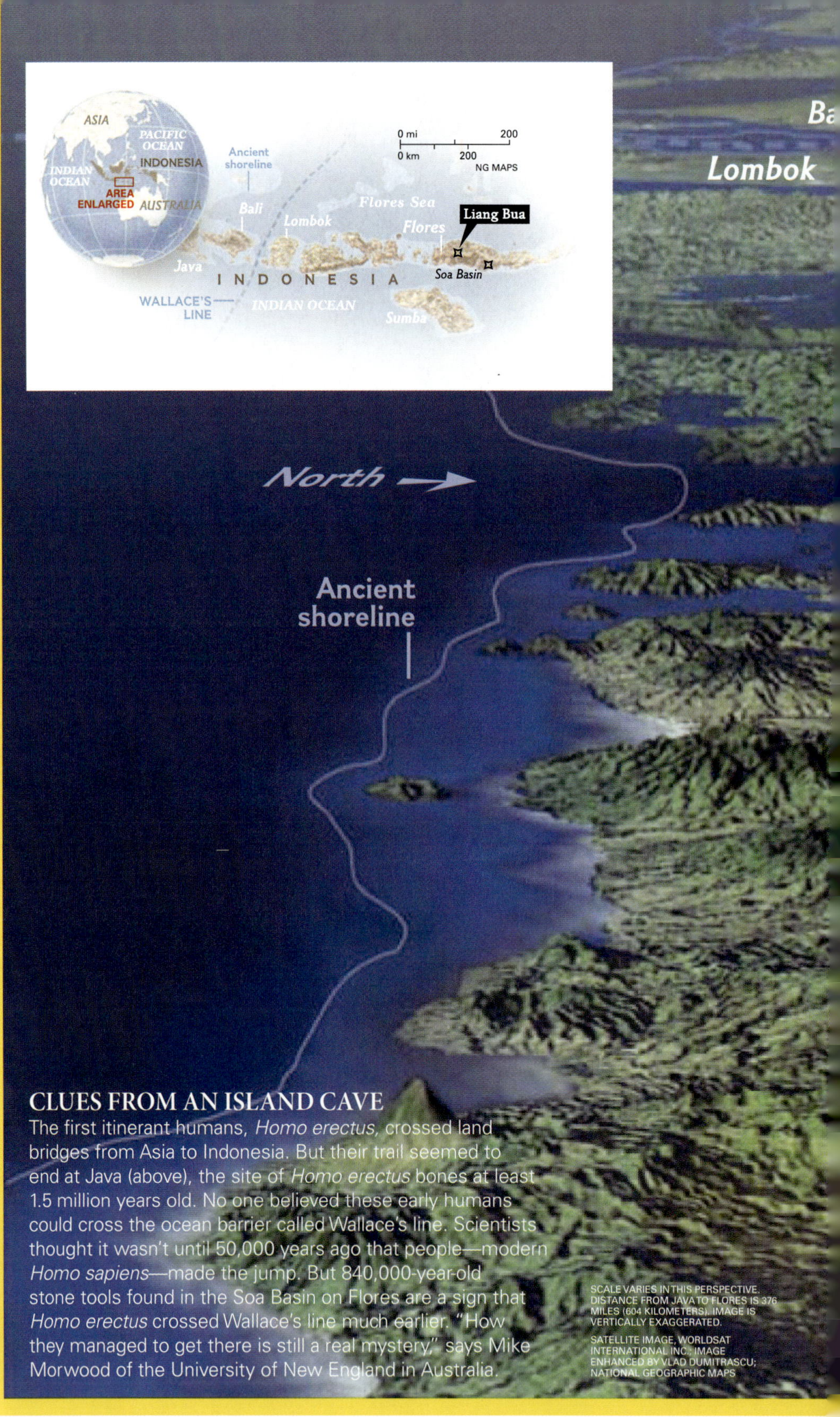

CLUES FROM AN ISLAND CAVE

The first itinerant humans, *Homo erectus*, crossed land bridges from Asia to Indonesia. But their trail seemed to end at Java (above), the site of *Homo erectus* bones at least 1.5 million years old. No one believed these early humans could cross the ocean barrier called Wallace's line. Scientists thought it wasn't until 50,000 years ago that people—modern *Homo sapiens*—made the jump. But 840,000-year-old stone tools found in the Soa Basin on Flores are a sign that *Homo erectus* crossed Wallace's line much earlier. "How they managed to get there is still a real mystery," says Mike Morwood of the University of New England in Australia.

WALLACE'S LINE
Sumbawa
Liang Bua
Flores
Basin

No ancient humans could have reached flores before big-brained modern people—or so it seemed. Looking for signs of early humans, archaeologists Wahyu Saptomo and Mike Morwood (right) examine stone artifacts found buried in a limestone cave that the local Manggarai people call Liang Bua. Above its massive entrance (bottom left) gray stalactites hang like jagged fangs, but the grim exterior belies an inner beauty. "It's very much like a cathedral inside," says Morwood, who has excavated here since 2001. He says islanders have used the cave as a burial ground for millennia. The dirt below its clay floor is riddled with human bones from a range of eras. But Morwood is interested in the cave's first occupants, *Homo floresiensis,* who arrived at least 95,000 years ago. The search has involved hauling tons of dirt bucket by bucket to a wash-ing station set up in a nearby rice field (top left), where researchers sifted artifacts and bones from the mud. The work paid off with the discovery of remains from at least seven tiny individuals. The team also found well-flaked stone points—possibly spearheads—that suggest *Homo floresiensis,* although much smaller than its Homo erectus ancestors, was also smarter.

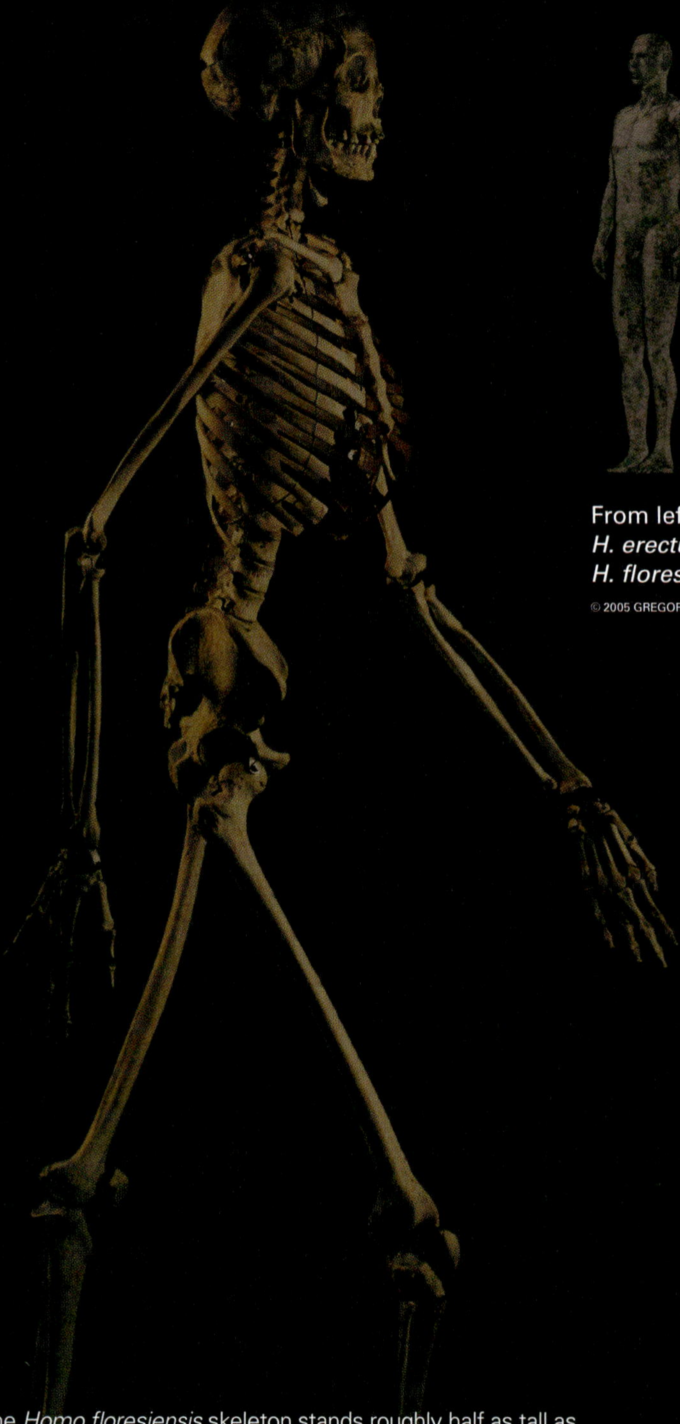

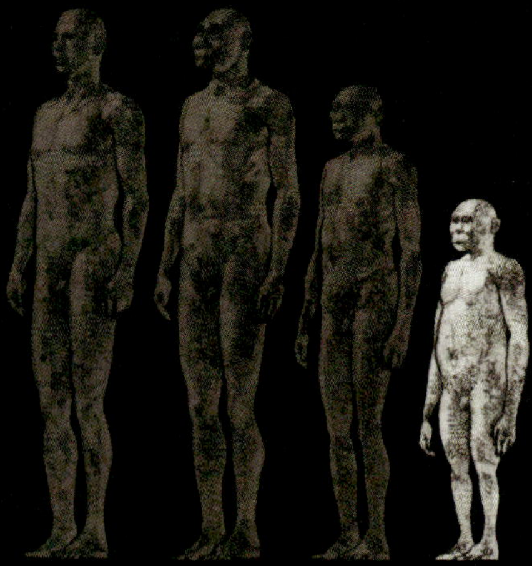

From left to right: *Homo sapiens, H. erectus, H. erectus (Dmanisi), H. floresiensis*

© 2005 GREGORY A. HARLIN/National Geographic Image Collection

The *Homo floresiensis* skeleton stands roughly half as tall as a modern adult's. "I knew within about 60 seconds of seeing the jawbone that this was something entirely new," says paleoanthropologist Peter Brown, who examined the bones. The premolars are a giveaway, with a root much different from ours. The pelvis of this female is also wider than in *Homo sapiens*. Her arms hung almost to her knees, says Brown, but her delicate hand and wrist bones imply that "she wasn't doing a lot of climbing."

© 2005 SNOWELL DESIGN & BALISTIC MEDIA/National Geographic Image Collection

WHERE DWARFS MET GIANTS

For millennia the only land mammals on flores were rodents, stegodonts, and humans.

Why were the Flores humans so small? Biogeographer Mark Lomolino, who studies the phenomenon called island dwarfism, says, "We know that when evolutionary pressures change, some species respond by shrinking." Stegodonts—extinct elephant ancestors—were especially prone to dwarfing, because they often colonized islands. "Elephants are strong swimmers," he says. Once there, with limited food and fewer predators, they shrank. On Sicily, Crete, and Malta, scientists have unearthed bones from primitive elephants as little as a twentieth the size of mainland forms. But other species, such as rats, tend to grow larger in a place without competitors. Flores yielded remains of giant rats and lizards, as well as cow-size dwarf stegodonts and diminutive human bones (shown above with stone tools and stegodont teeth). Peter Brown says the tiny Homo floresiensis may have evolved from a population of Homo erectus that reached Flores some 800,000 years ago. "The problem is we haven't found Homo erectus bones," says Brown. "All we have is these small-bodied people."

FLORES WALKING SKELETON ART (LEFT) BY MARK SNOSWELL, SAM HODGE, AND DAMIAN SNELGROVE, SNOSWELL DESIGN & BALLISTIC MEDIA; ART (TOP LEFT AND RIGHT) BY GREG HARLIN; SOURCES (TOP LEFT): H. SAPIENS, CHRISTOPHER B. RUFF; H. ERECTUS, SUSAN C. ANTÓN AND CONNIE FELLMAN

Brown rat and flores giant rat

Asian elephant and liang bua stegodont

Water monitor and komodo dragon

ASIAN ODYSSEY

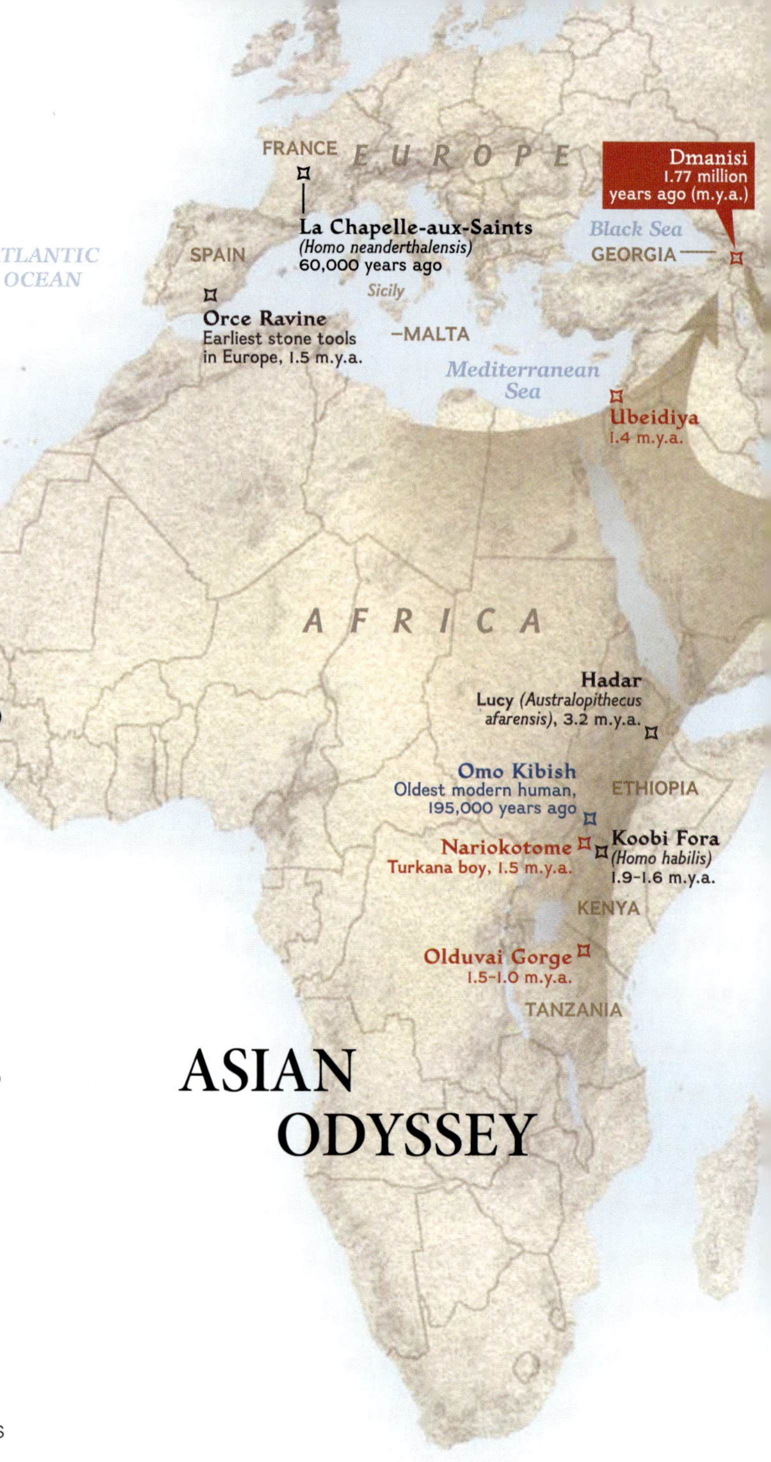

TWO SPECIES SEPARATED BY 1.8 MILLION YEARS AND 6,000 MILES. ARE THEY DISTANT COUSINS?

In analyzing the bones of a tiny human relative called Hobbit, from the Indonesian island of Flores, scientist Peter Brown noted that they looked more like *Homo erectus* remains recently found at Dma-nisi in western Asia than like *Homo erectus* from nearby Indonesian islands. "That's very weird," he says. Much research must be done to determine if the two species are linked. For now, the finds are adding to the picture of early human diasporas. Dmanisi shows that human ancestors left Africa earlier than was thought and that these wanderers had adopted a carnivore's protein-laden diet. Meat-eating may have been key to survival outside Africa, and it may have set human ancestors on an evolutionary course to larger brains, typical of predators. Meanwhile, Flores suggests hominins crossed stretches of ocean much earlier than scientists believed, leading scholars to wonder about other unknown human species. "*Homo erectus* may have reached many Indonesian islands and evolved," says Richard Roberts of Australia's University of Wollongong. "We may be in for more surprises."

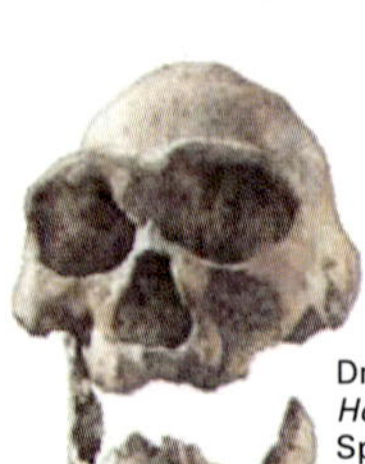

Dmanisi
Homo erectus
Specimen D3444
1.77 million years old

2 million years ago — 1.5 m.y.a

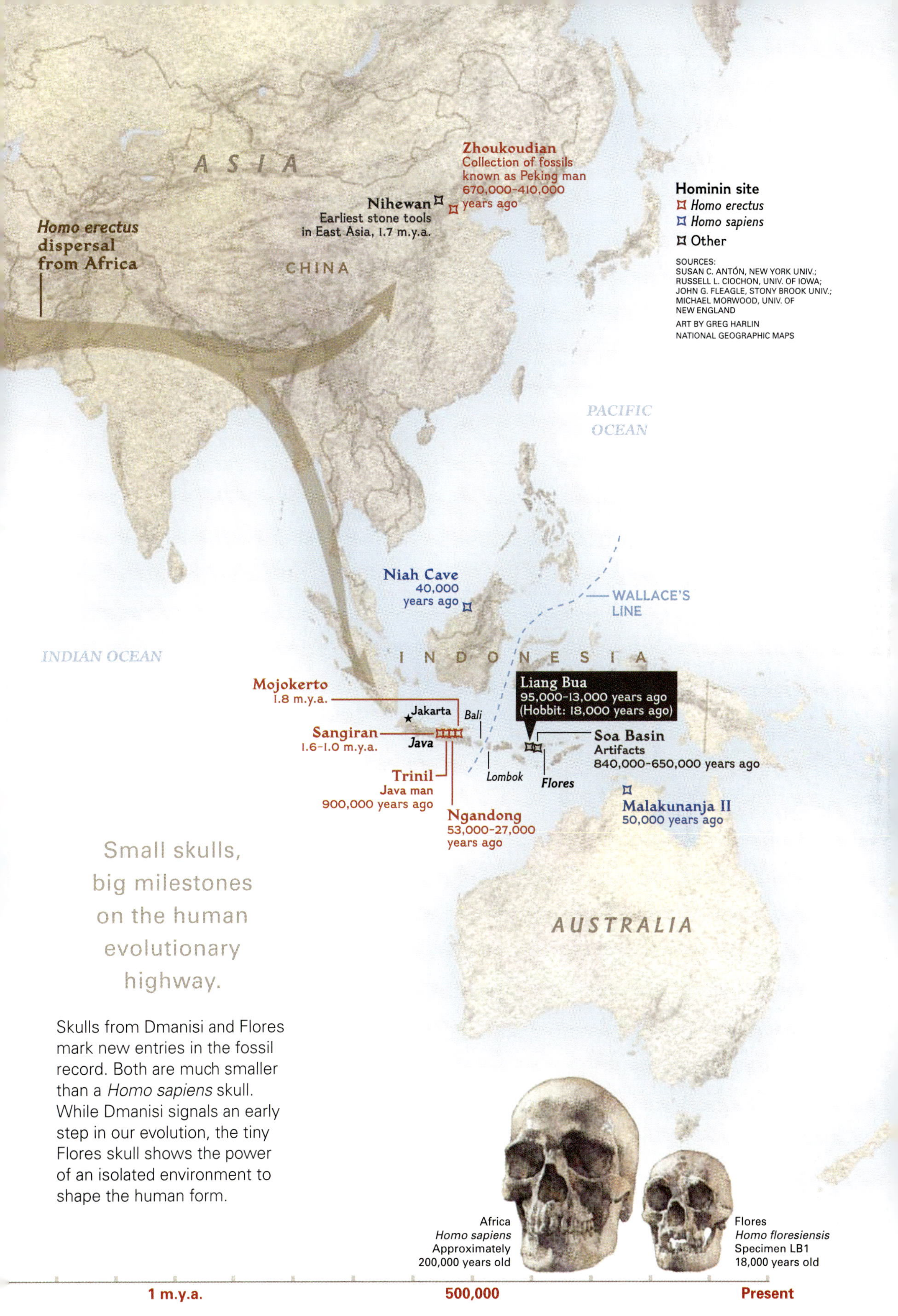

Small skulls, big milestones on the human evolutionary highway.

Skulls from Dmanisi and Flores mark new entries in the fossil record. Both are much smaller than a *Homo sapiens* skull. While Dmanisi signals an early step in our evolution, the tiny Flores skull shows the power of an isolated environment to shape the human form.

(Continued from page 73) Yet in the 1950s and '60s Theodor Verhoeven, a priest and part-time archaeologist, had found signs of an early human presence. In the Soa Basin of Flores he found stone artifacts near stegodont fossils, thought to be around 750,000 years old. Homo erectus, an archaic hominin (a term for humans and their relatives), was known to have lived on nearby Java at least 1.5 million years ago, so Verhoeven concluded that erectus somehow crossed the sea to Flores.

Perhaps modern humans did meet their ancient neighbors before something spelled the end for the little people.

As an amateur making extraordinary claims, Verhoeven failed to persuade the archaeological establishment. In the 1990s, however, other researchers used modern techniques to date tools from the Soa Basin to about 840,000 years ago. Verhoeven was right: Human ancestors had reached Flores long before modern humans landed. But no actual remains of Flores's earlier inhabitants had ever turned up.

So we went looking, focusing on Liang Bua, in the uplands of western Flores. By September 2003 our team of Indonesian and Australian researchers, assisted by 35 Manggarai workers, had dug 20 feet into the cave floor. Younger layers were rich in stone artifacts and animal bones, but by this point the dig seemed played out.

Then, a few days before the three-month exca-vation was due to end, our luck changed. A slice of bone was the first hint. The top of a skull appeared next, followed by the jaw, pelvis, and a set of leg bones still joined together—almost the entire skeleton of Hobbit.

We knew we had made a stunning discovery, but we didn't dare remove the bones for a closer look. The waterlogged skeleton was as fragile as wet blotting paper, so we left it in place for three days to dry, applied a hardener, then excavated the remains in whole blocks of deposit.

Cradled in our laps, the skeleton accompanied us on the flight back to Jakarta, Indonesia's capital. There Peter Brown, a paleoanthropologist from the University of New England in Australia, supervised cleaning, conservation, and analysis. The pelvic structure told him Hobbit was a female, and her tooth wear confirmed that she was an adult. Her sloping forehead, arched browridges, and nutcracker jaw resembled those of Homo erectus, but her size was unique.

It wasn't just her small stature and estimated weight—about 55 pounds—but a startlingly small brain as well. Brown calculated its volume at less than a third of a modern human's. Hobbit had by far the smallest brain of any member of the genus Homo. It was small even for a chimpanzee.

The tiny skull is most reminiscent not of the hefty Homo erectus from elsewhere in East Asia but of older, smaller erectus fossils. Viewed from above, the skull is pinched in at the temples, a feature also seen in the 1.77-million-year-old Dmanisi people from Georgia, in western Asia. And in some respects, such as the shape of her lower jaw, the Liang Bua hominin harks back to even earlier fossils such as Lucy, the 3.2-million-year-old Australopithecus from Ethiopia.

And yet—strangest of all—she lived practically yesterday. Radiocarbon dating of charcoal pieces found next to the skeleton, together with luminescence dating that indicated when the surrounding sediments were last exposed to the sun, revealed her 18,000-year age. By mid-2004 our excavation at Liang Bua had yielded bones and teeth from at least six other individuals, from about 95,000 until as recently as 13,000 years ago.

For a few skeptics, all this is too much to swallow. They argue that the one complete skull must have come from a modern human with a rare condition called microcephaly, in which the brain is shrunken and the body dwarfed. The other small bones, they say, might be the remains of children. But last year's discoveries include part of a

An imagined encounter between a modern human and a tiny Flores human. No definitive evidence has emerged that the two species met, but scientists think they coexisted for some 40,000 years.

second adult skull—a lower jaw—that is just as small as the first. It simply strains credibility to invoke a rare disease a second time.

Instead, Hobbit is our first glimpse of an entirely new human species: Homo floresiensis. Her kind probably evolved from an earlier Homo erectus population, likely the makers of the tools Verhoeven found. Her ancestors may have stood several feet taller at first. But over hundreds of thousands of years of isolation on Flores, they dwindled in size.

Such dwarfing is often the fate of large mammals marooned on islands. There they generally face fewer predators—on Flores, Komodo dragons were the only threat—which makes size and strength less important. And the scarce food resources on a small island turn a large, calorie-hungry body into a liability. On mainland Asia, stegodonts sometimes grew bigger than African elephants; at Liang Bua they were only a bit bigger than present-day water buffalo.

In the past some anthropologists have argued that even in prehistory humans could adapt to new environments by inventing new tools or behaviors rather than by physically evolving, like other creatures. The dwarfing seen on Flores is powerful evidence that humans aren't exempt from natural selection. The discovery of Hobbit is also a hint that still other human variants may once have inhabited remote corners of the world.

In spite of their downsized brains, the little people apparently had sophisticated technology. The fireplaces, charred bones, and thousands of stone tools we found among their remains must have been their handiwork, for we found no sign of modern humans. Stone points, probably once hafted onto spears, turned up among stegodont bones, some of which bore cut marks. The little hominins were apparently hunting the biggest animals around. It was surely a group activity—adult stegodonts, although dwarfed, still weighed more than 800 pounds, formidable prey for hunters the size of preschool children.

The discovery underscores a puzzle going back to Theodor Verhoeven: How could ancient hominins ever have reached Flores? Was Homo erectus a better mariner than anyone suspected, able to build rafts and plan voyages? And it raises a new and haunting question. Modern humans colonized Australia from mainland Asia about 50,000 years ago, populating Indonesia on their way. Did they and the hobbits ever meet?

There's no sign of modern humans at Liang Bua before 11,000 years ago, following a large volcanic eruption that would have wiped out any Homo floresiensis in the region. But other bands may have hung on elsewhere in Flores. Perhaps modern humans did meet their ancient neighbors before something—maybe a changing environment, maybe competition or conflict with modern humans themselves—spelled the end for the little people. Further excavations on Flores, and on nearby islands that might have had their own hobbits, may settle the question.

In the meantime a clue may come from local folktales about half-size, hairy people with flat foreheads—stories the islanders tell even today. It's breathtaking to think that modern humans may still have a folk memory of sharing the planet with another species of human, like us but unfathomably different.

The Australian Research Council supported this work; your Society will help sponsor future study.

Discussion Questions

- Name at least five peculiarties of the *H.* floresiensis finds.
- How do physical anthropologists explain the appearance of *H.* floresiensis on the island of Flores? How do they explain their Hobbit-like size?
- To what proposed species of *Homo* is floresiensis related? What physical resemblances exist between them? How do they differ?
- As the article indicates, *H.* floresiensis' brains are relatively small even for chimpanzees. Despite this, what

technologies are they reported to have used?

Join the Debate

Scientists in opposition of *H. floresiensis* as a new species argue that microcephaly or other pathological conditions are more likely to explain the small size of cranium LB1 (the only *H. floresiensis* cranium to date). In 2009, Falk et al. compared 3D virtual endocasts (internal braincases) of LB1 to those of normal humans, microcephalic humans, *H. erectus* and gamut of other hominids and primates. While their findings are premature of ruling out all genetic syndromes connected to downsized crania, their results reject the possibility of microcephaly and, instead, propose a neurological reorganization that would have allowed for sophisticated tool use despite their small brain size[1].

Access the article at your local eLibrary and examine the endocasts.

- Which casts does LB1 most resemble?
- What does the strong reaction against the new species imply about our perceptions of brain size and intelligence?
- In what ways do the remains and associated artifacts of *H. floresiensis* force us to rethink our evolutionary past?

Field Journal

Search the web for images of crania with Microcephaly, Laron's Syndrome, and Cretinism and compare them to *H. florensis* LB1. Observe the frontal (forehead), parietal (top side), temporal (side) and occipital (back) lobes of the cranium. Based on this visual examination, how likely are you to identify LB1 as having a genomic syndrome? How else might you interpret LB1?

---

[1] *Dean Falk, Charles Hildebolt, Kirk Smith, M.J. Morwood, Thomas Sutikna, Jatmiko, E. Wayhu Saptomo, Fred Prior. (2009). "LB1's Virtual Endocast, Microcephaly, and Hominin Brain Evolution."* Journal of Human Evolution *57(5): 597–607.*

THE DOWNSIDE OF UPRIGHT

This article looks at the biomechanics of upright bipedalism and its associated morphological changes for gait efficiency. In the equilibrium of anatomical change—particularly of the spine, pelvis, knee joint, and foot—"evolutionary compromises" that afforded us bipedalism simultaneously brought about biomechanical flaws that explain modern-day musculoskeletal ailments. Comparisons are made with our primate brethren and hominid progenitors.

As you read "The Downside of Upright," consider the following questions:

- What changes in the skeleton took place to support upright posture and bipedalism?
- What are the common ailments associated with bipedalism?

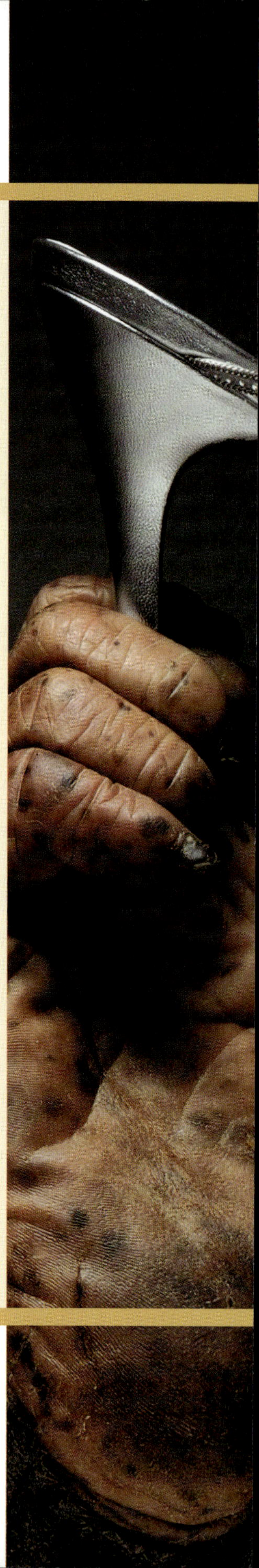

Homely but highly dexterous, a chimp's flat feet have strong, thumblike opposable toes that allow for climbing, grasping, and fingering a berry—or a beautiful but impractical shoe. Our bipedal ancestors gave up all this in favor of rigid, arched, hyper-specialized feet prone to many ills.

THE DOWNSIDE OF UPRIGHT

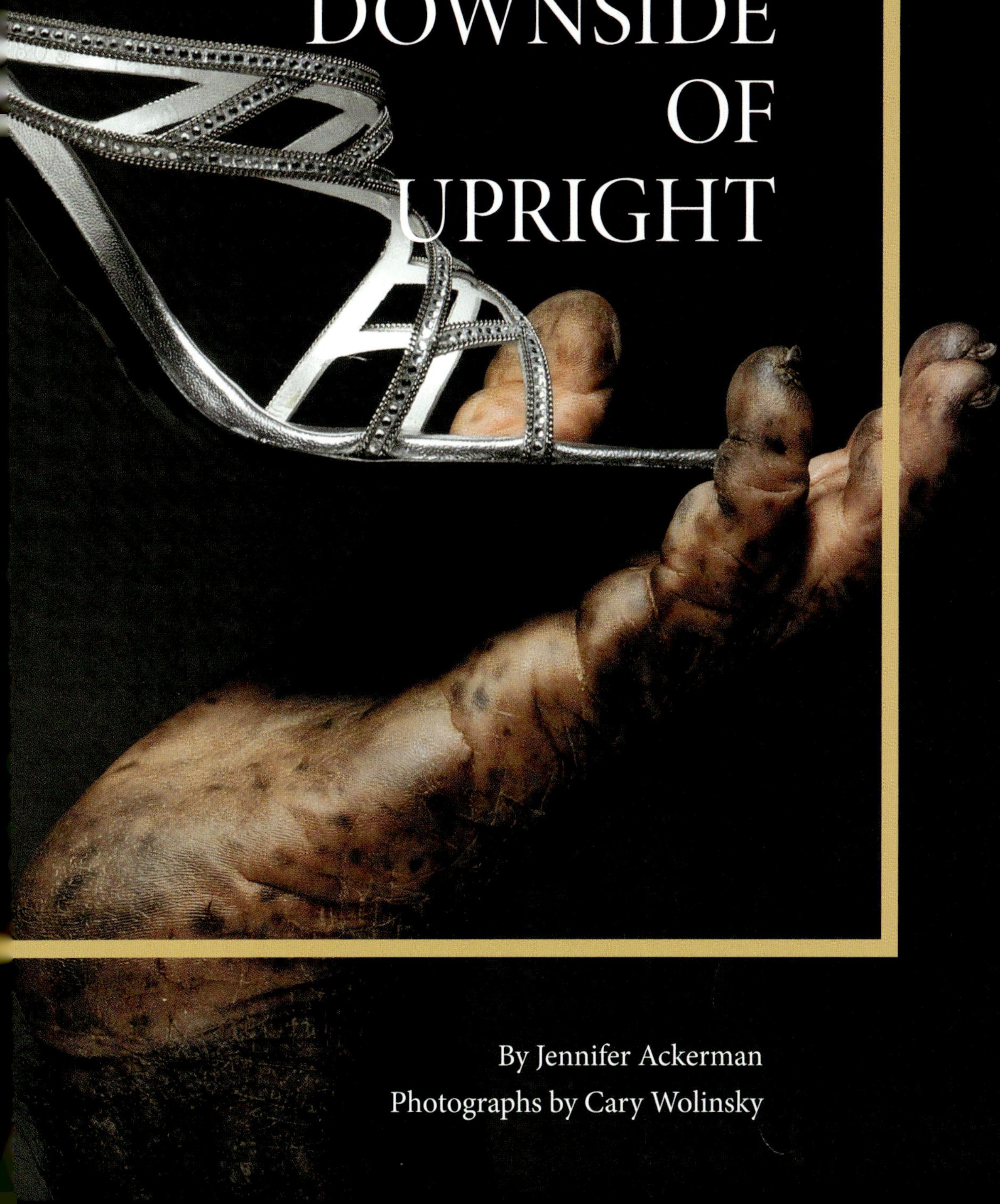

By Jennifer Ackerman
Photographs by Cary Wolinsky

Marvin Lipschutz, a 63-year-old physician who suffered from a herniated, or slipped, vertebral disk, hangs on an inversion table designed to relieve back pain and pressure, a technique dating back to Hippocrates in 400 B.C. Today, roughly 80 percent of adults experience back problems sometime in their lives—a consequence of our upright posture. Humans have likely suffered this way since our ancestors first stood up, transforming our backbone from a bridge or arch to a column that must bear the full weight of the upper body. Especially vulnerable is the lower, or lumbar, region of the column, where pressure on the disks that separate our vertebrae can cause them to bulge or herniate.

THE AGILITY AND BRAINPOWER WE'VE GAINED SINCE OUR ANCESTORS STOOD UP ON TWO FEET HAVEN'T COME WITHOUT EVOLUTIONARY TRADE-OFFS:

A PLETHORA OF ACHES AND PAINS THAT MAKE IT HARD TO BE HUMAN.

We humans are odd creatures: tailless bipeds with sinuous spines, long limbs, arched feet, agile hands, and enormous brains. Our bodies are a mosaic of features shaped by natural selection over vast periods of time—both exquisitely capable and deeply flawed. We can stand, walk, and run with grace and endurance, but we suffer aching feet and knee injuries; we can twist and torque our spines, and yet most of us are plagued by back trouble at some point in our lives; we can give birth to babies with big brains, but only through great pain and risk. Scientists have long sought to answer the question of how our bodies came to be the way they are. Now, using new methods from a variety of disciplines, they are discovering that many of the flaws in our "design" have a common theme: They arise primarily from evolutionary compromises that came about when our ancestors stood upright—the first step in the long path to becoming human.

They arise primarily from evolutionary compromises that came about when our ancestors stood upright—the first step in the long path to becoming human.

A Tight Squeeze

In Karen Rosenberg's laboratory at the University of Delaware, a room packed with the casts of skulls and bones of chimpanzees, gibbons, and other primates, one model stands out: It's a life-size replica of a human female pelvic skeleton mounted on a platform. There is also a fetal skull with a flexible gooseneck wire. The idea is to simulate the human birth process by manually moving the fetal head through the pelvis.

It looks easy enough.

"Go ahead, try it," Rosenberg says.

Turn the little oval skull face-forward, and it drops neatly into the pelvic brim, the beginning of the birth canal. But then it jams against the protrusions of the ischial bones (those that bear the burden during a long car ride). More shoving and rotating, and it's quickly apparent that the skull must

---

Adapted from "The Downside of Upright" by Jennifer Ackerman: National Geographic Magazine, July 2006.

traverse a passage that seems smaller than itself, cramped not only by the ischial bones but also by the coccyx, the bottom of the tailbone, which pokes into the lower pelvic cavity. Only by maneuvering the skull to face sideways in the middle of the canal and then giving it a firm push, does it move a centimeter or two—before it gets hung up again. Twist it, jostle it: The thing won't budge. Rosenberg guides my hand to turn the skull around to face backward, and then, with a hard shove, the stubborn cranium finally exits the birth canal.

"Navigating the birth canal is probably the most gymnastic maneuver most of us will ever make in life," says Rosenberg, chair of the university's department of anthropology. It's a trick all right, especially if there's no guiding hand to twirl and ram the skull. And the neat two-piece model doesn't even include the broad, rigid shoulders of the human infant, a legacy from our apelike ancestors who, some 20 million years ago, evolved wide clavicles that allowed them to hang suspended from branches and feed on fruit. To follow the head, a baby's shoulders must also rotate two times to work through the birth canal; they sometimes get stuck, causing injury to part of the spinal nerves that control the arms.

Suddenly I understand as never before why it took 36 hours, two doctors, and three shifts of nurses to safely deliver my firstborn.

Birth is an ordeal for women everywhere, according to a review of birthing patterns in nearly 300 cultures around the world by Rosenberg and colleague Wenda Trevathan, an anthropologist at New Mexico State University. "Not only is labor difficult," Rosenberg says, "but because of the design of the female pelvis, infants exit the birth canal with the back of their heads against the pubic bones, facing in the opposite direction from the mother. This makes it tough for her to reach down and guide the baby as it emerges without damaging its spine—and also inhibits her ability to clear the baby's breathing passage or to remove the umbilical cord from around its neck. That's why women everywhere seek assistance during labor and delivery."

Compared with humans, most primates have an easier time, Rosenberg says. A baby chimpanzee, for instance, is born quickly: entering, passing through, and leaving its mother's pelvis in a straight shot and emerging faceup so that its mother can pull it forward and lift it toward her breast. In chimps and other primates, the oval birth canal is oriented the same way from beginning to end. In humans, it's a flattened oval one way and then it shifts orientation 90 degrees so that it's flattened the other way. To get through, the infant's head and shoulders have to align with that shifting oval. It's this changing cross-sectional shape of the passageway that makes human birth difficult and risky, Rosenberg says, not just for babies but also for mothers. A hundred years ago, childbirth was a leading cause of death for women of childbearing age.

Why do we possess a birth canal of such Byzantine design? "The human female pelvis is a classic example of evolutionary compromise," Rosenberg answers. Its design reflects a trade-off between the demand for a skeletal structure that allows for habitual walking on two feet and one that permits the passage of a baby with a big brain and wide shoulders. Its unique features didn't come about all at once, but at different times in our evolutionary history, in response to different selective pressures. "The result of these different pressures is a jerry-rigged, unsatisfactory structure," Rosenberg says. "It works, but only marginally. It's definitely not the type of system you would invent if you were designing it. But evolution is clearly a tinkerer, not an engineer; it has to work with yesterday's model."

Yesterday's Model

Humans come from a long line of ancestors, from reptile to mammal to ape, whose skeletons were built to carry their weight on all fours. Our ape ancestors probably evolved around 20 million years ago from small primates that carried themselves horizontally. Over the next several million years, some apes grew larger and began to use their arms to hold overhead branches and, perhaps, to reach for fruit. Then, six or seven million years ago, our ancestors stood up and began to move about on their hind legs. By the time the famous Lucy (Australo-pithecus afarensis) appeared in East Africa 3.2 million years ago, they had adopted walking as their chief mode of getting around.

It was a radical shift. "Bipedalism is a unique and bizarre form of locomotion," says Craig Stanford, an anthropologist at the University of Southern California. "Of more than 250 species of primates, only one goes around on two legs." Stanford and many other scientists consider bipedalism the key defining feature of being human. "Some may think it's our big brain," Stanford says, "but the rapid expansion of the human brain didn't begin until less than two million years ago, millions of years after we got upright and began using tools. Bipedalism was the initial adaptation that paved the way for others."

Evolutionary biologists agree that shifts in behavior often drive changes in anatomy. Standing upright launched a cascade of anatomical alterations. The biomechanics of upright walking is so drastically different from quadrupedal locomotion that bones from the neck down had to change. The skull and spine were realigned, bringing the head and torso into a vertical line over the hips and feet. To support the body's weight and absorb the forces of upright locomotion, joints in limbs and the spine enlarged and the foot evolved an arch. As for the pelvis: It morphed from the ape's long, thin paddle into a wide, flat saddle shape, which thrust the weight of the trunk down through the legs and accommodated the attachment of large muscles. This improved the stability of the body and the efficiency of walking upright but severely constricted the birth canal.

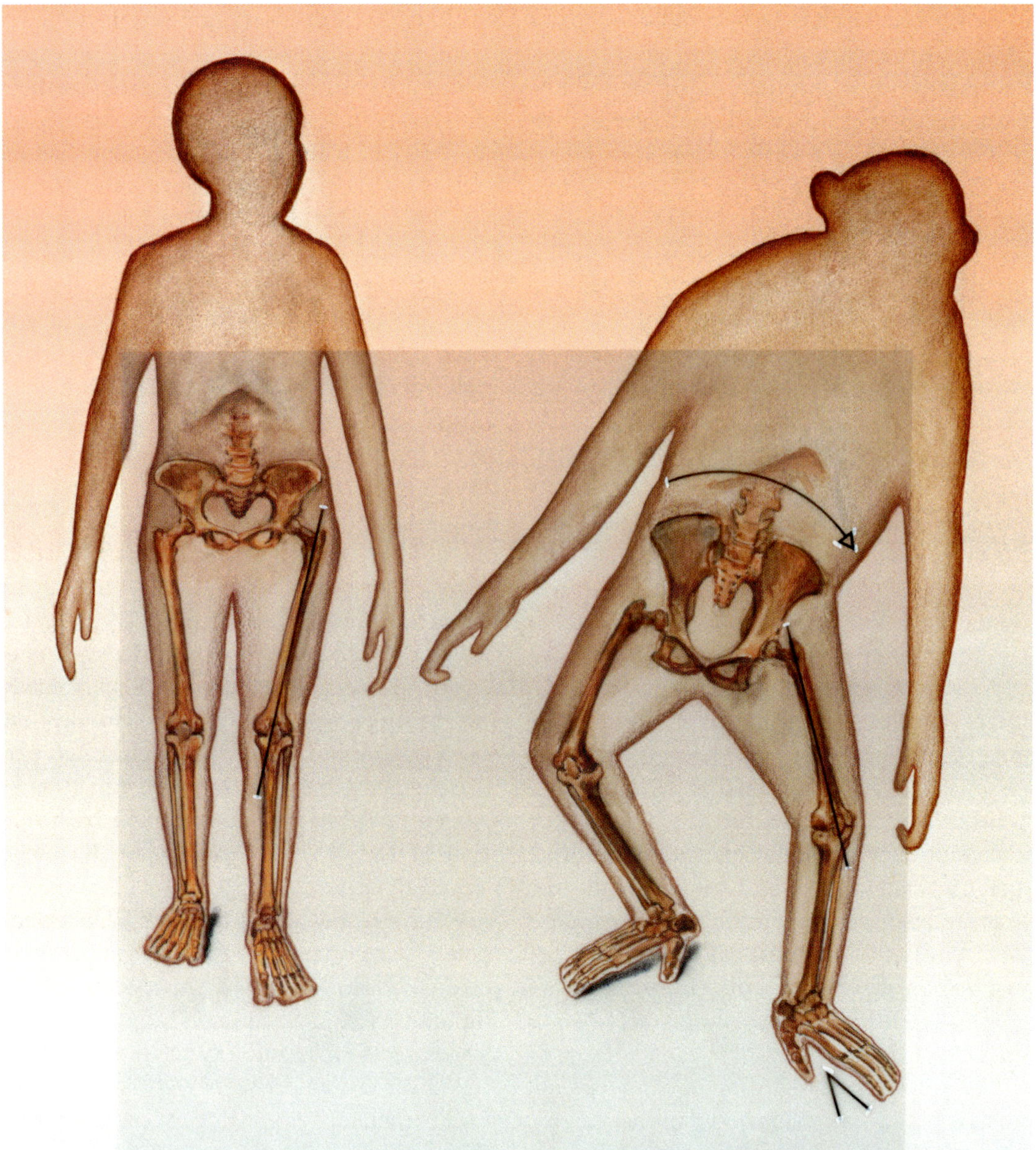

ANCESTRAL GAIT

A dynamic 3-D computer model created at the University of Liverpool shows a skeleton walking with a chimplike bent-hip-bent-knee gait. The model, programmed with the proportions of the famous Australopithecus afarensis *fossil, Lucy, suggests that this gait would have put such high energy demands on her knees and ankles that she would have rapidly overheated. Researchers believe that this hominin evolved a different, more erect, and more efficient gait.*

© 1985 JICHA, JON/National Geographic Image Collection

All of these architectural changes, seen clearly in the fossil record, did not happen overnight. They came gradually, over many generations and over long periods of time, in small steps favored by natural selection.

Upright Citizens

Consider the simple human act of walking or running. At his laboratory in the anthropology department at Harvard University, Dan Lieberman does just that, using biomechanical studies to see how we use our body parts in various aspects of movement. As a volunteer subject in one of his experiments last fall, I was wired up and put through paces on a treadmill. On my feet were pressure sensors to show my heel and toe strikes. Electromyographic sensors revealed the firing of my muscles, and accelerometers and rate gyros on my head detected its pitching, rolling, and yawing movements. Small silver foam balls attached to my joints—ankle, knee, hip, elbow, shoulder—acted as reflectors for three infrared cameras mapping in three-dimensional space the location of my limb segments.

Bipedalism is a unique and bizarre form of locomotion. Of more than 250 species of primates, only one goes around on two legs.

These biomechanical windows on walking and running illuminate just how astonishing a feat of balance, coordination, and efficiency is upright locomotion. The legs on a walking human body act not unlike inverted pendulums. Using a stiff leg as a point of support, the body swings up and over it in an arc, so that the potential energy gained in the rise roughly equals the kinetic energy generated in the descent. By this trick the body stores and recovers so much of the energy used with each stride that it reduces its own workload by as much as 65 percent.

The key lies in our human features: the ability to fully extend our knees; the way our lower back curves forward and our thighbone slopes inward from hip to knee so that our feet straddle our center of gravity; and the action of the gluteal abductors, the muscles attached to the pelvis that contract to prevent us from toppling over sideways mid-stride when our weight is on a single foot.

In running, we shift from this swinging pendulum mode to a bouncy pogo-stick mode, using the tendons in our legs as elastic springs. Lieberman's recent studies with Dennis Bramble of the University of Utah suggest that running—which our ancestors mastered some two million years ago—was instrumental in the evolution of several features, including our extra leg tendons, our relatively hairless skin and copious sweat glands (which facilitate cooling), and our enlarged gluteus maximus, the biggest muscle in the body, which wraps the rear end and acts to stabilize the trunk, preventing us from pitching forward. Now Lieberman is studying the role in upright locomotion of a tiny slip of muscle in the neck called the cleidocranial trapezius—all that remains of a massive shoulder muscle in chimps and other apes—which steadies our head during running, preventing it from bobbling.

Watching the graphs from the experiment on a computer screen, one can't help but marvel at the effectiveness of the system, the little cleidocranial portion of the trapezius steadying the head; the regular pumping action of arms and shoulders stabilizing the body; the consistent springlike rhythms of our long-legged stride.

"Compare this with the chimp," Lieberman says. "Chimps pay a hefty price in energy for being built the way they are. They can't extend their knees and lock their legs straight, as humans can. Instead, they have to use muscle power to support their body weight when they're walking upright, and they waste energy rocking back and forth."

Chimps are our closest living evolutionary relatives and, as such, are especially well suited to teach us about ourselves. Almost every bone in a chimp's body correlates with a bone in a human body. Whatever skeletal distinctions exist are primarily related to the human pattern of walking upright—hence the keen interest in parsing these distinctions among those who study the origins of human bipedalism.

Two-legged walking in a chimp is an occasional, transitory *(Continued on page 96)*

Was walking on two legs an energy-saving measure for our ancestors? To help scientists fathom the answer, a trained, ten-year-old chimpanzee named Louie ambles willingly on a treadmill, first on two legs, and then on all four, his more usual "knuckle-walking" gait. The loose-fitting flow-through mask captures his exhalations, which scientists analyze to measure energy expenditure. White dots on his joints convey to cameras the location and movement of his limbs in space. By revealing the amount of energy Louie expends with each step and how it's used, such experiments may shed light on the energetics of our chimplike forebears—and whether energy economy was a likely catalyst for their shift to bipedalism several million years ago.

(Continued from page 93) behavior. In humans, it is a way of life, one that carries with it myriad benefits, perhaps chief among them, freed hands. But upright posture and locomotion come with a host of uniquely human maladies.

Achilles' Back

An old friend of mine, a former politician from West Virginia, has difficulty remembering names. He saves himself from embarrassment with a simple trick: He delivers a hearty handshake and asks, "So how's your back?" Four times out of five he strikes gold. Names become unnecessary when the acquaintance, flattered by the personal inquiry, launches into a saga of lumbar pain, slipped disk, or mild scoliosis.

Back pain is one of the most common health complaints, accounting for more than 15 million doctor visits each year. That most of us will experience debilitating back pain at some point in our lives raises the question of the spine's design.

"The problem is that the vertebral column was originally designed to act as an arch," explains Carol Ward, an anthropologist and anatomist at the University of Missouri in Columbia. "When we became upright, it had to function as a weight-bearing column." To support our head and balance our weight directly over our hip joints and lower limbs, the spine evolved a series of S curves—a deep forward curve, or lordosis, in the lower back, and a backward curve, or kyphosis, in the upper back.

This change took place at least four million years ago, probably much earlier. Ward and her colleague Bruce Latimer, director of the Cleveland Museum of Natural History, recently analyzed the vertebral column of Lucy, along with two Australopithecus africanus skeletons from more than two million years ago. They found that the spines of all three possess the same S curves present in the human spine, confirming that Australopithecus walked on two legs.

"This system of S curves is energetically efficient and effective for maintaining our balance and for bipedal locomotion," Ward says. "But the lower region of the column suffers from the excessive pressure and oblique force exerted on its curved structure by our upright posture."

Lean back, arching your spine. You're the only mammal in the world capable of this sort of backbend. Feel a cringing tightness in your lower back? That's the vertical joints between your vertebrae pressing against one another as their compressive load increases. The curvature in your lower spine requires that its building blocks take the shape of a wedge, with the thick part in the front and the thin part in the back. The wedge-shaped vertebrae are linked by vertical joints that prevent them from slipping out from one another.

"These joints are delicate structures and very complex," Ward says. "They allow our spines to move with great flexibility, to twist and bend and flex, pivoting on the disks between the vertebrae."

But in the lower back region, where the load is heaviest and the wedging most dramatic, strains such as heavy lifting or hyperextension (say, from doing the butterfly stroke or cleaning the gutters) can cause your lowest vertebrae to slip or squish together. When the vertebrae are pressured in this way, the disks between them may herniate, or bulge out, impinging on spinal nerves and causing pain. Or the pressure may pinch the delicate structures at the back of the vertebrae, causing a fracture called spondylolysis, a problem for about one in twenty Americans.

No other primate experiences such back problems—except, Ward and Latimer say, our immediate ancestors. The two scientists have found fossil evidence that back trouble likely plagued our bipedal forebears. The bones of the Nariokotome boy, a young Homo erectus (a species preceding our own Homo sapiens) who lived some 1.5 million years ago, reveal that the youth suffered from scoliosis, a potentially devastating lateral curvature of the spine.

The cause of most scoliosis cases remains a mystery, Latimer says, but like spondylolysis, it appears linked to the spinal features associated with upright posture, particularly lordosis, the deep forward curvature and flexibility of our lower spine. "Because scoliosis occurs only in humans and our immediate bipedal ancestors, it appears likely that upright walking is at least partially to blame," he says.

The rapid expansion of the human brain didn't begin until less than two million years ago, millions of years after we got upright.

Considering the pressures of natural selection, why are such seriously debilitating diseases still prevalent? Latimer suspects the answer lies in the importance of lordosis for upright walking: "Selection for bipedality must have been so strong in our early ancestors that a permanent lordosis developed despite the risk it carries for spondylolysis and other back disorders."

Disjointed

Liz Scarpelli's postural orientation is at the moment horizontal. Her leg is elevated in a surgical sling as Scott Dye, an orthopedic surgeon at California Pacific Medical Center, examines her knee with an arthroscope. The ghostly image of the joint—femur, tibia, and patella—appear magnified on a flat screen above the gurney. An athletic woman of 51, a former gymnast and skier, Scarpelli is a physical therapist who works with patients to rehabilitate their joints after surgery. While demonstrating to one patient a technique for leg-strengthening knee squats, Scarpelli blew out her own knee for the third time. Dye's arthroscopic camera shows healthy bone and ligaments, but large chunks of cartilage float about like icebergs in the fluid spaces around the joint. Dye expertly scrapes up the pieces and sucks them out before sewing up the holes and moving on to the next five surgeries scheduled for the day.

To hear Scott Dye speak of it, the knee joint is among the greatest of nature's inventions, "a 360-million-year-old structure beautifully designed to do its job of transferring load between limbs." But it is also among the most easily injured joints in the human body; medical procedures involving knees total a million a year in the United States.

"In standing upright, we have imposed unprecedented forces on the knee, ankle, and foot," Bruce Latimer says. When we walk quickly or run, the forces absorbed by our lower limbs may approach several multiples of our own body weight. Moreover, our pelvic anatomy exerts so-called lateral pressure on our lower joints. Because of the breadth of our pelvis, our thighbone is angled inward toward the knee, rather than straight up and down, as it is in the chimp and other apes. This carrying angle ensures that the knee is brought well under the body to make us more stable.

"But nothing is free in evolution," Latimer says. "This peculiar angle means that there are forces on the knee threatening to destabilize it. In women, the angle is greater because of their wider pelvis, which explains why they are slower runners—the increased angle means that they're wasting maybe ten percent of their energy—and also why they tend to suffer more knee injuries."

Unlikely Feat

And where does the buck finally stop? What finally bears the full weight of our upright body? Two ridiculously tiny platforms.

"The human foot has rightfully been called the most characteristic peculiarity in the human body," says Will Harcourt-Smith, a paleontologist at the American Museum of Natural History. "For one thing, it has no thumblike opposable toe. We're the only primate to give up the foot as a grasping organ."

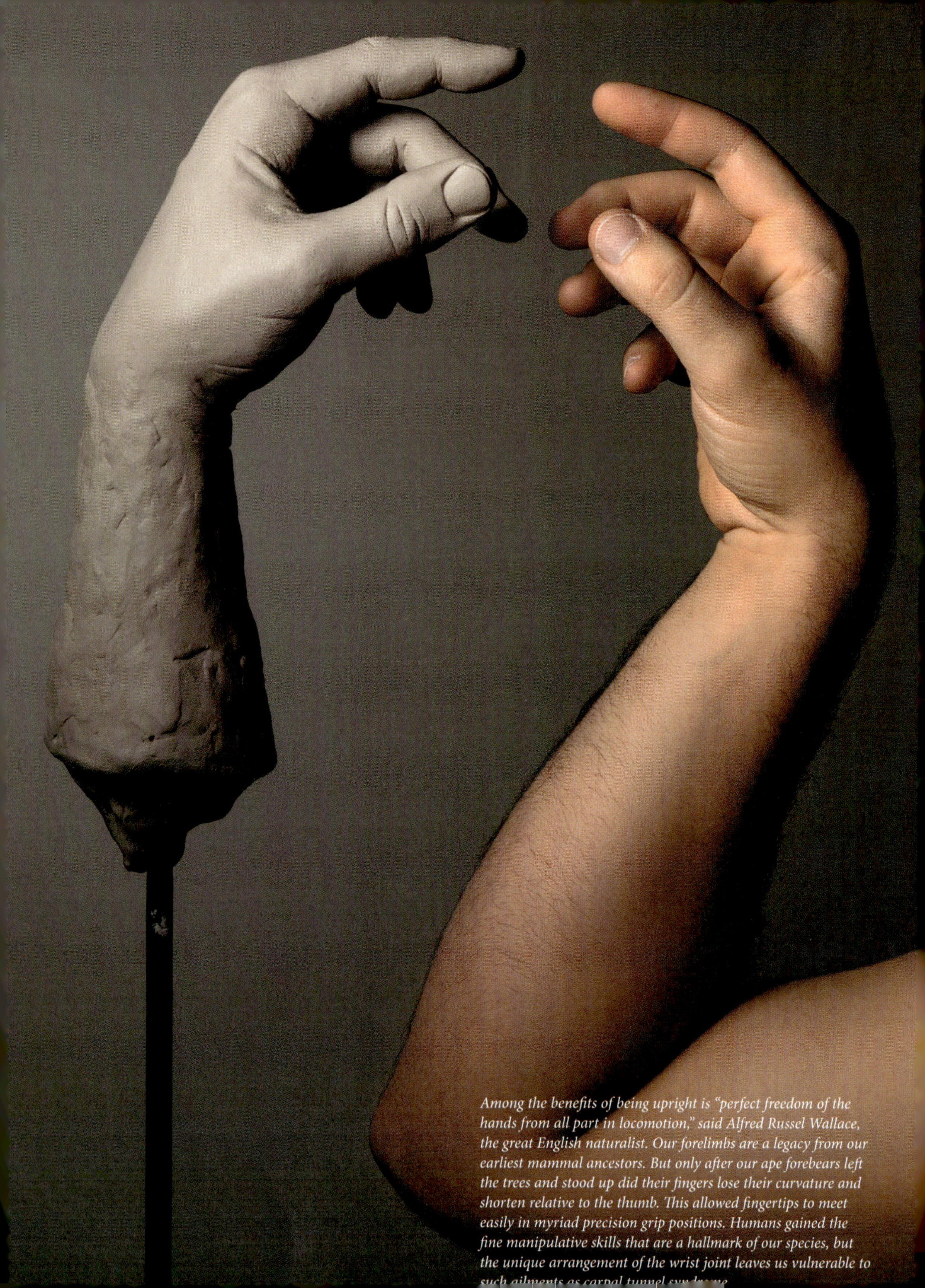

Among the benefits of being upright is "perfect freedom of the hands from all part in locomotion," said Alfred Russel Wallace, the great English naturalist. Our forelimbs are a legacy from our earliest mammal ancestors. But only after our ape forebears left the trees and stood up did their fingers lose their curvature and shorten relative to the thumb. This allowed fingertips to meet easily in myriad precision grip positions. Humans gained the fine manipulative skills that are a hallmark of our species, but the unique arrangement of the wrist joint leaves us vulnerable to such ailments as carpal tunnel syndrome.

This was a huge sacrifice. The chimp's foot is a brilliantly useful and versatile feature, essential to tree climbing and capable of as much motion and manipulation as its hand. The human foot, by contrast, is a hyper-specialized organ, designed to do just two things, propel the body forward and absorb the shock of doing so. Bipedality may have freed the hands, but it also yoked the feet.

Harcourt-Smith studies foot bones of early hominins with the new technique of geometric morphometrics—measuring objects in three dimensions. The variations in foot structure he has discovered in Australopithecus and Homo habilis (a species that lived 2.5 to 1.6 million years ago) suggest that these early hominins may have walked in different ways.

"We have a desire to see the story of bipedalism as a linear, progressive thing," he says, "one model improving on another, all evolving toward perfection in Homo sapiens. But evolution doesn't evolve toward anything; it's a messy affair, full of diversity and dead ends. There were probably lots of ways of getting around on two feet."

Still, in all the fossil feet Harcourt-Smith studies, some type of basic human pattern is clearly present: a big toe aligned with the long axis of the foot, or a well-developed longitudinal arch, or in some cases a humanlike ankle joint—all ingenious adaptations but fraught with potential problems. "Because the foot is so specialized in its design," Harcourt-Smith says, "it has a very narrow window for working correctly. If it's a bit too flat or too arched, or if it turns in or out too much, you get the host of complications that has spurred the industry of podiatry." In people with a reduced arch, fatigue fractures often develop. In those with a pronounced arch, the ligaments that support the arch sometimes become inflamed, causing plantar fasciitis and heel spurs. When the carrying angle of the leg forces the big toe out of alignment, bunions may form—more of a problem for women than men because of their wider hips.

And that's not all.

"One of the really remarkable aspects of the human foot, compared with the chimp and other apes, is the relatively large size of its bones, particularly the heel bone," Bruce Latimer notes. "A 350-pound male gorilla has a smaller heel bone than does a 100-pound human female—however, the gorilla bone is a lot more dense." While the ape heel is solid with thick cortical bone, the human heel is puffed up and covered with only a paper-thin layer of cortical bone; the rest is thin latticelike cancellous bone. This enlargement of cancellous bone is pronounced not just in the heel, but in all the main joints of our lower limbs—hip, ankle, knee—and has likely marked the skeleton of our ancestors since they first got upright; it has been found in the joints of 3.5-million-year-old hominin fossils from Ethiopia.

"The greater volume of bone is an advantage for dissipating the stresses delivered by normal bipedal gait," Latimer says. However, it's not without cost: "The redistribution in our bones from cortical to cancellous means that humans have much more surface exposure of their skeletal tissue. This results in an accelerated rate of bone mineral loss—or osteopenia—as we age, which may eventually lead to osteoporosis and hip and vertebral fractures."

What Do We Stand For?

We humans gave up stability and speed. We gave up the foot as a grasping tool. We gained spongy bones and fragile joints and vulnerable spines and difficult, risky births that led to the deaths of countless babies and mothers. Given the trade-offs, the aches and pains and severe drawbacks associated with bipedalism, why get upright in the first place?

A couple of chimps named Jack and Louie may offer some insights. The chimps are part of an experiment by a team of scientists to explore the origin of bipedalism in our hominin ancestors. *(Continued on page 102)*

Upside-down and ready to deliver, a human fetal skull facing rear—in position for birth—points out perhaps the greatest downside of being upright: a difficult passage through the bony canal of a female pelvis. So tight is the fit that the human fetus must rotate as it moves down the canal; in some cases its cranial bones must squeeze together and overlap, compressing the skull a few millimeters so the infant can exit. The challenging nature of human birth reflects a history of compromise between the demands of bipedalism and a big brain. As our pelvis narrowed and our brain expanded, more than doubling in size from two million years to 100,000 years ago, the fit grew even tighter. The solution: Humans are born with their brains only a quarter of adult size.

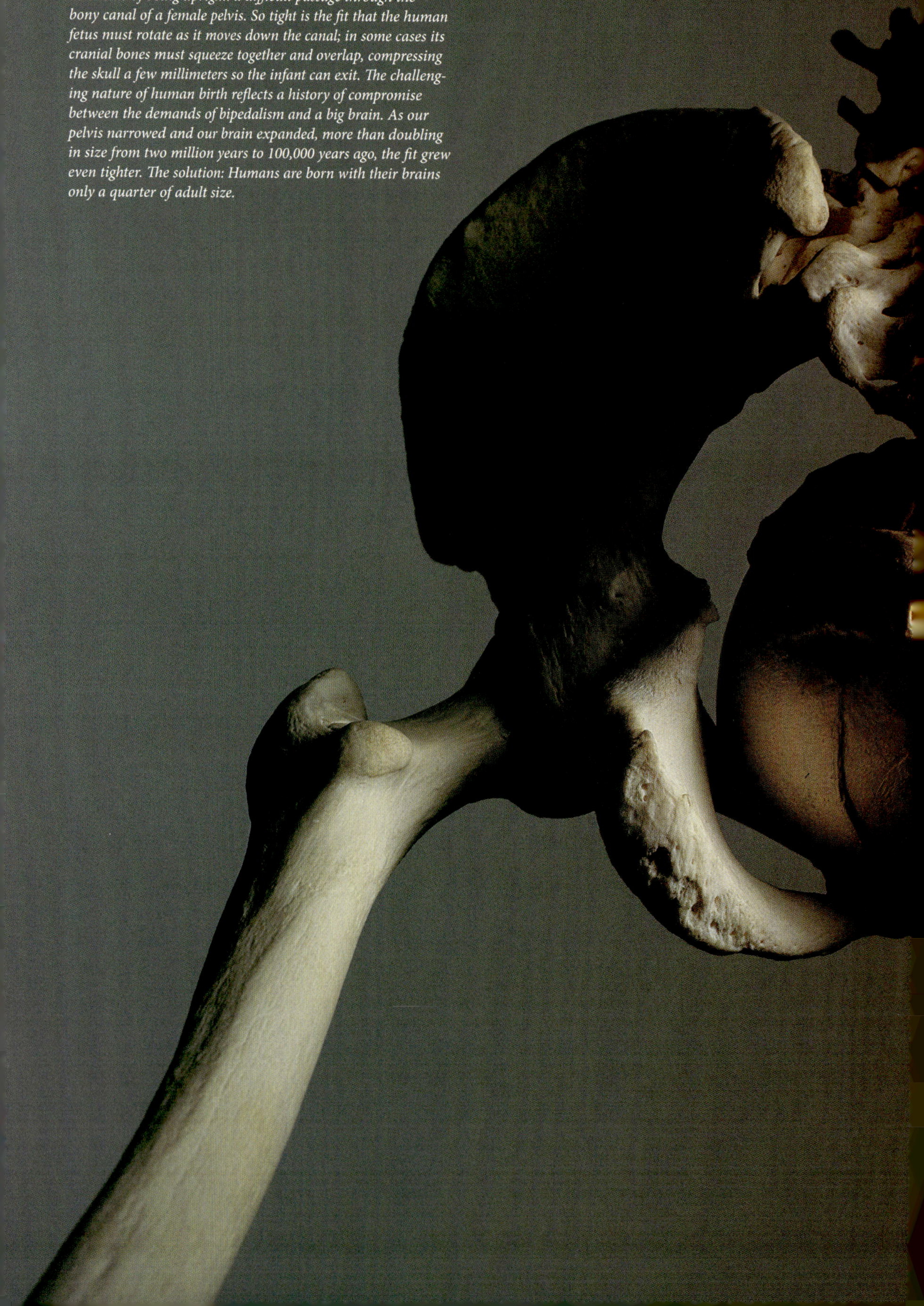

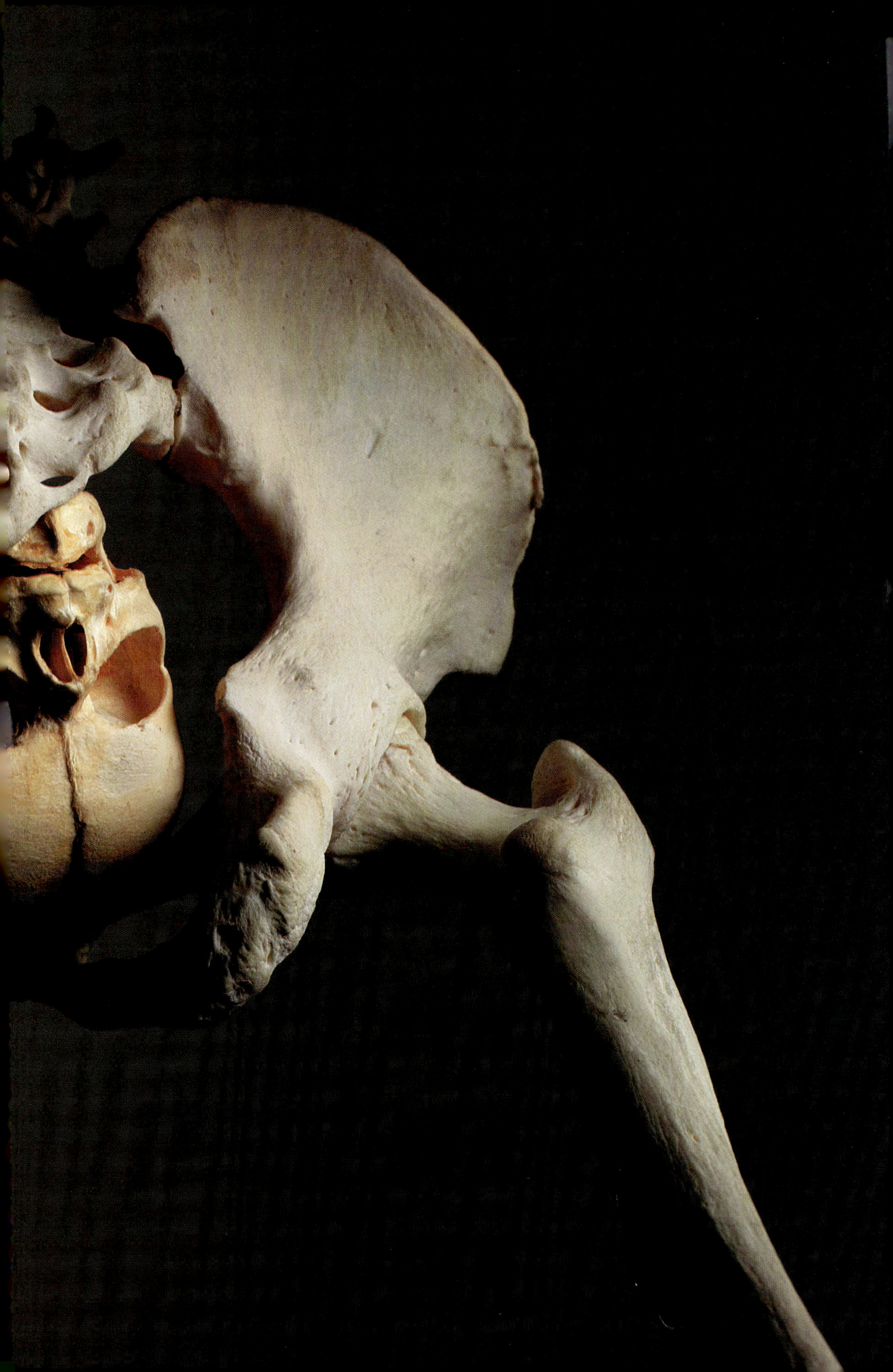

(Continued from page 99) Theories about why we got upright have run the gamut from freeing the arms of our ancestors to carry babies and food to reaching hitherto inaccessible fruits. "But," says Mike Sockol of the University of California, Davis, "one factor had to play a part in every scenario: the amount of energy required to move from point to point. If you can save energy while gathering your food supply, that energy can go into growth and reproduction."

> **It's definitely not the type of system you would invent if you were designing it. But evolution is clearly a tinkerer, not an engineer.**

Paleogeographical studies suggest that at the time our ancestors first stood upright, perhaps six to eight million years ago, their food supplies were becoming more widely dispersed. "Rainfall in equatorial East Africa was declining," Sockol says, "and the forest was changing from dense and closed to more open, with more distance between food resources. If our ape ancestors had to roam farther to find adequate food, and doing so on two legs saved energy, then those individuals who moved across the ground more economically gained an advantage."

To test the theory that the shift to two feet among our ancestors may have been spurred by energy savings, Sockol and his colleagues are looking at the energy cost of locomotion in the chimp. The chimp is a good model, Sockol says, not just because it's similar to us in body size and skeletal features and can walk both bipedally and quadrupedally, but also because the majority of evidence suggests that the last common ancestor of chimps and humans who first stood upright was chimplike. By understanding how a chimp moves, and whether it expends more or less energy in walking upright or on all fours (knuckle-walking), the scientists hope to gain insight into our ancestors' radical change in posture.

Jack and Louie and several other young adult chimps have been trained by skillful professional handlers to walk and run on a treadmill, both on two legs and on four. One morning, Jack sits patiently in his trainer's lap while Sockol's collaborators, Dave Raichlen and Herman Pontzer of Harvard University, paint small white patches on his joints—the equivalent of those silver balls I wore on Dan Lieberman's treadmill. Only occasionally does Jack steal a surreptitious lick of the sweet white stuff. Once he's marked, he jumps on the treadmill and runs along on two legs for a few minutes, then drops to four. Every so often, his trainer hands him a fruit snack, which Jack balances on his lower lip, thrust out as far as it will go, before rolling the fruit forward and flicking it into his mouth. For a set time, Jack breathes into a small mask connected to equipment that gathers information on how much oxygen he consumes—a measure of energy expenditure—while the movements of his limbs (marked by those white dots, see pages 94–95) are monitored with cameras to help the scientists understand how the energy is being used.

Once the scientists have refined their model for how things work in the chimp—for what limb movements are used in the two types of locomotion and how each consumes energy—they hope to apply this model to the fossils of our ancestors. "We use the biomechanical data to determine the types of anatomical changes that would have reduced energy expenditure," Raichlen explains. "Then we look at the fossil record and ask, Do we see these changes? If we do, that's a pretty good clue that we're looking at selection for reduced energy costs in our ancestors who became bipedal. That's the dream."

Scientists are the first to admit that much work needs to be done before we fully

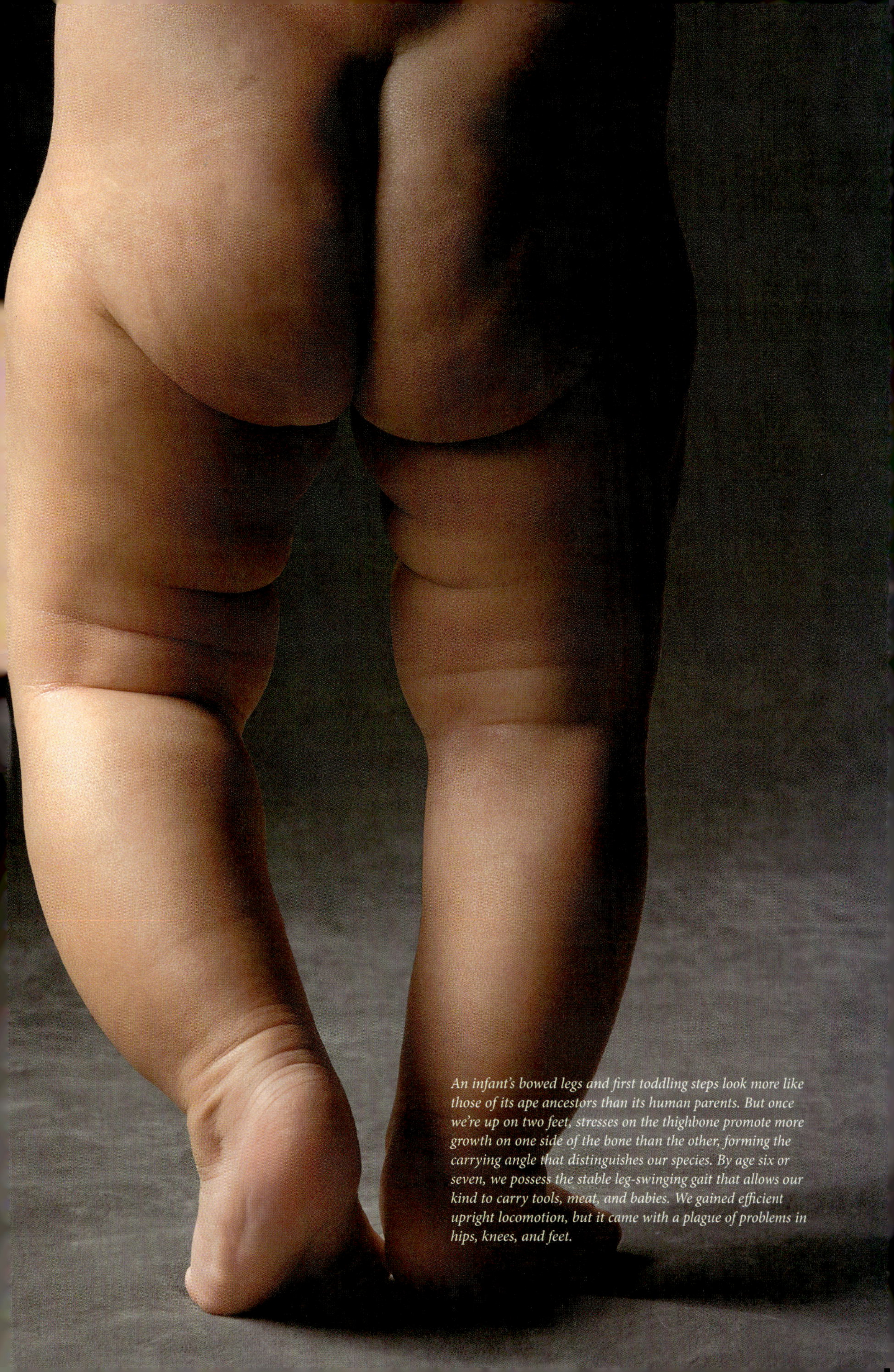

An infant's bowed legs and first toddling steps look more like those of its ape ancestors than its human parents. But once we're up on two feet, stresses on the thighbone promote more growth on one side of the bone than the other, forming the carrying angle that distinguishes our species. By age six or seven, we possess the stable leg-swinging gait that allows our kind to carry tools, meat, and babies. We gained efficient upright locomotion, but it came with a plague of problems in hips, knees, and feet.

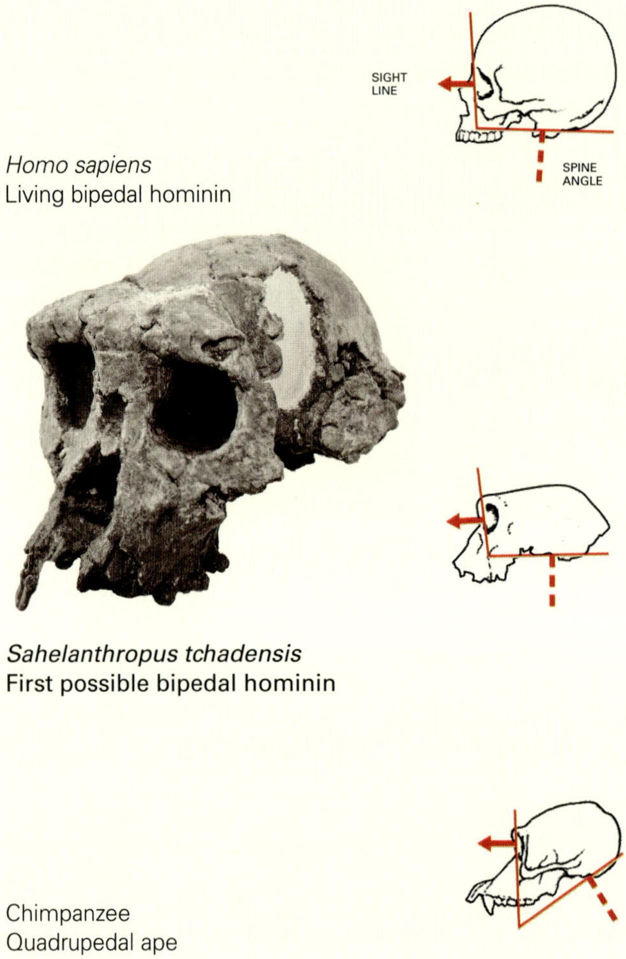

HEADS UP

A hole in the head offers a clue to the beginnings of bipedalism. In modern humans the intersection of the plane of the foramen magnum—the hole where the spine enters the skull—and the plane associated with the eye sockets forms nearly a right angle. In chimps the angle is more acute. The Sahelanthropus tchadensis *fossil was crushed when found, but a computer reconstruction shows an angle close to perpendicular, suggesting to some scientists that the species, perhaps the oldest hominin, stood upright.*

© Greg Harlin/NGM Art/National Geographic Image Collection

SOURCES: © MISSION PALEOANTHROPOLOGIQUE FRANCO-TCHADIENNE (MIDDLE).

understand the origins of bipedalism. But whatever drove human ancestors to get upright in the first place—reaching for fruit or traveling farther in search of it, scanning the horizon for predators or transporting food to family—the habit stuck. They eventually evolved the ability to walk and run long distances. They learned to hunt and scavenge meat. They created and manipulated a diverse array of tools. These were all essential steps in evolving a big brain and a human intelligence, one that could make poetry and music and mathematics, assist in difficult childbirth, develop sophisticated technology, and consider the roots of its own quirky and imperfect upright being.

Discussion Questions

- What skeletal elements are involved with bipedal locomotion and what muscular changes can you infer from the evolution of quadrupedalism to bipedalism? What muscles are reduced and what muscles are enlarged?
- What "evolutionary compromises" are associated with modern-day birthing complications, spondylitis, runner's knee, and heel spurs?
- According to fossil evidence, *A. africanus* also possessed the S-curve of the spine, which indicates bipedalism. What morphological differences, then, explain the differences in modern human bipedalism and that of our upright hominid ancestors?
- How might you explain the spongy and porous bones of humans and the dense bones of the great apes?

Join the Debate

As mentioned in this article, "Evolutionary biologists agree that shifts in behavior often drive changes in anatomy" (91). While we are subject to "evolutionary compromises," how might modern medicine, physical therapy, organic and processed diets, activity level, and the use of technology (e.g., cars, text messaging, and laptops) impact the trajectory of human evolution?

Field Journal

Visit www.eSkeletons.org and www.eFossils.org. Compare the os coxa (one side of the pelvis) of a human, gorilla, chimp, and *A.* afarensis for the following: its overall articulation with the whole skeleton, width, height, bone density, and angle of articulation with the femur (when possible). What differences do you note between bipeds, occasional bipeds, and quadrupeds?